Better Homes and Gardens®

kitchens

Meredith® Books
Des Moines, Iowa

Better Homes and Gardens® *Kitchens*
Editor: Paula Marshall
Project Manager/Writer: Catherine Staub, The Lexicon Group
Contributing Editors: Julie Collins, Dave Remund, The Lexicon Group
Graphic Designer: David Jordan, Studio 22
Copy Chief: Terri Fredrickson
Publishing Operations Manager: Karen Schirm
Senior Editor, Asset and Information Manager: Phillip Morgan
Edit and Design Production Coordinator: Mary Lee Gavin
Editorial Assistant: Kaye Chabot
Book Production Managers: Pam Kvitne, Marjorie J. Schenkelberg, Rick von Holdt, Mark Weaver
Contributing Copy Editor: Wendy Wetherbee
Contributing Proofreaders: Dan Degan, Pam Elizian, Jeanee LeDoux
Cover Photographer: Emily Followill
Indexer: Kathleen Poole

Meredith® **Books**
Executive Director, Editorial: Gregory H. Kayko
Executive Director, Design: Matt Strelecki
Executive Editor/Group Manager: Denise Caringer
Marketing Product Manager: Tyler Woods

Publisher and Editor in Chief: James D. Blume
Editorial Director: Linda Raglan Cunningham
Executive Director, New Business Development: Todd M. Davis
Executive Director, Sales: Ken Zagor
Director, Operations: George A. Susral
Director, Production: Douglas M. Johnston
Director, Marketing: Amy Nichols
Business Director: Jim Leonard

Vice President and General Manager: Douglas J. Guendel

Better Homes and Gardens® **Magazine**
Editor in Chief: Karol DeWulf Nickell
Deputy Editor, Home Design: Oma Blaise Ford

Meredith Publishing Group
President: Jack Griffin
Executive Vice President: Bob Mate

Meredith Corporation
Chairman and Chief Executive Officer: William T. Kerr
President and Chief Operating Officer: Stephen M. Lacy

In Memoriam: E.T. Meredith III (1933-2003)

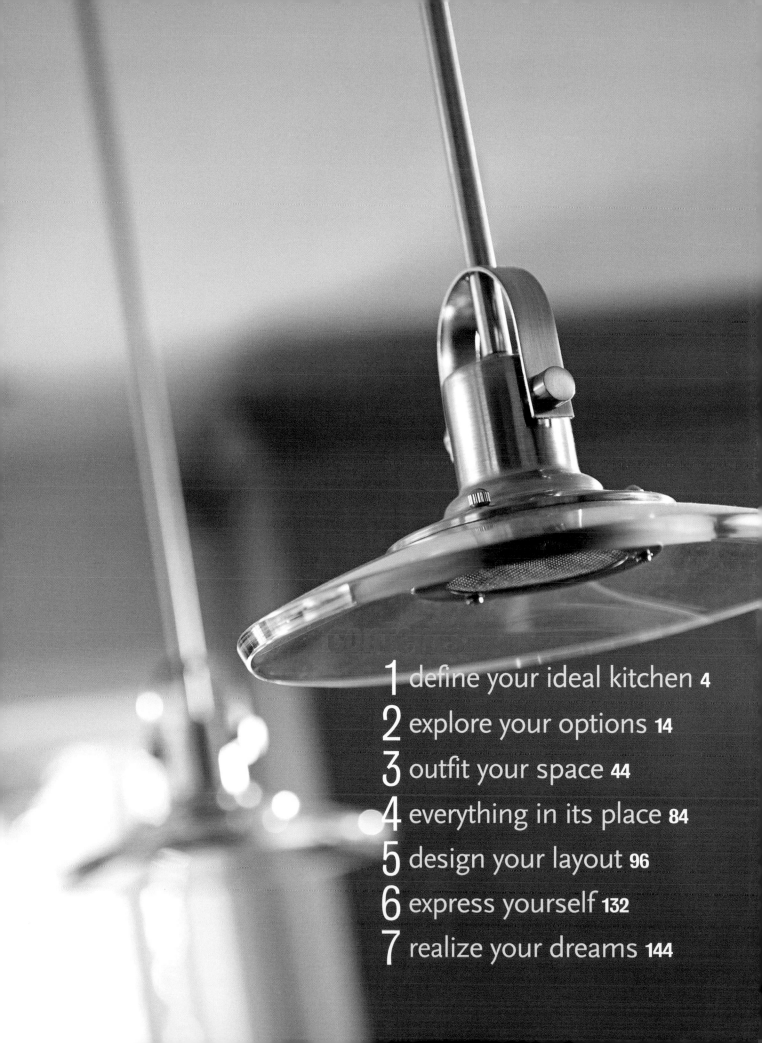

contents

define your ideal kitchen

Creating the perfect space to welcome family and friends into your home starts with a list of your needs and desires. »

When you're in the planning stage of remodeling a kitchen, focus on the problems you want to fix. You may discover better solutions than you initially imagined. If you have a tight budget, you probably will need to prioritize which issues are the most critical to resolve. Or with smart planning, solve all the pressing problems and then prioritize amenities.

assess your needs

WHAT'S IN YOUR KITCHEN?

Ask yourself the following questions and you'll get a better picture of what you already have, what you need, and what you want from your kitchen. If the kitchen is used equally by your spouse or partner, answer the questions together.

- How much time do you spend in your kitchen?
- What are you doing when you're there? Are you eating meals, reading, relaxing, or working on projects? Do you use the phone or computer there?
- Who's in the kitchen with you? Children, friends, family, or colleagues?
- How does your kitchen make you feel when you're in it? How would you like it to make you feel?
- If you wrote "A Day in the Life of My Kitchen," how would it read? Would it be different on weekends or holidays? Would it be different three to five years from now?
- Do you cook alone? If you cook with others, how many share the space?
- What do you cook? Elaborate, all-day dishes or simple, quick meals?
- How many people do you regularly cook for? How often do you cook for a different number of people?
- Do you have special cooking interests, such as baking or grilling?
- What large and small appliances do you use? Are they sufficient? Any special storage needs?
- What appliances do you use simultaneously?
- Do you have plenty of workspace for your kitchen activities? Is this space where you'd like it?
- Is your storage space for equipment and ingredients adequate and in a place that works for you? Can you find everything easily?
- Is your kitchen comfortable for you to work in? Why or why not?
- Does your kitchen's arrangement cause you physical strain? What adjustments would be most helpful?
- Does your kitchen work well for everyone who uses it? Do you have any children or other family members with specific height requirements or other needs?

WHAT'S IN PLACE?

In almost every kitchen begging for an overhaul, an asset or two is waiting to be appreciated. Let this question simmer for a few days as you discover the best aspects of your kitchen space. Do you have a high ceiling or a roomy floor plan? Do you have access to a great view, even if it's limited by a tiny window or none at all? Are your appliances in good shape? Do you have spaces, such as closets or small rooms, near the kitchen that are underused and therefore offer potential for a kitchen expansion? Your answers may present opportunities for your kitchen that you'd never imagined possible.

MAKING A WISH LIST

Creating your dream kitchen is in the details. In addition to determining your basic needs, give yourself permission to write a wish list. With careful planning—particularly when you work with a design professional—you may be surprised at how many of your dreams can become reality while you remain true to your budget. What makes a kitchen ideal is highly personal. Keep in mind the overall size of your kitchen. You may better achieve your dream by going with standard materials and appliances and

spending extra money to annex space from an adjoining room. Finally, consider upgrades to surface materials, cabinets, and appliances.

In addition to the basics, envision a kitchen including some or all of the following:

Amenities:
- Food storage: lazy Susans, spice drawers, pullout pantry
- Dish storage: pots-and-pans drawers, platter slots, baking sheet slots, secondary storage for seasonal dishes
- Linen storage
- Pet food storage and eating area
- Shelves for cookbooks
- Garden area: potting sink, greenhouse window
- Recycling area

Appliances:
- Convection oven
- Warming drawers
- Refrigerator drawers
- Wine cooler
- Second dishwasher
- Triple-bowl sink
- Secondary prep sink
- Trash compactor
- Water purifier
- Washer/dryer

ABOVE: **New box windows, removed partitions, and angled dishwasher placement opened up the potential of this kitchen. Daylight contributes to the illusion of roominess, making the galley seem wider.**

finding inspiration

Your personal style may be consistent from your choice of clothing to the decoration of your home, or it may vary widely depending on the situation or your mood. Whether your style is traditional, contemporary, country, retro, artistic, or reflective of a favorite vacation spot—or an eclectic mix of these—remember that you'll be in your kitchen every day. How much time do you want to spend cleaning or maintaining the space? Do you like an uncluttered look, or do you want your kitchen equipment out and around you?

You may be updating your existing kitchen for practical reasons. Perhaps dated appliances barely function or a changing family situation means more time can be devoted to gourmet meal preparation. Whatever your reasons, before selecting any appliances or fixtures, even before setting the budget, think about style. You needn't be overly specific; just focus on images and words that convey the abiding intent of your kitchen project: a welcoming family gathering spot, a sleek professional cook's dream, a spot for entertaining,

RIGHT: **Tired of conventional kitchens, the homeowners took inspiration for this industrial-style cooking space from commercial kitchens. Restaurant-style shelves above the cooktop keep necessities visible and handy.**

home central, soothing colors, quiet repose, traditional elegance, contemporary drama—whatever suits you. Once practicalities enter the picture, truly indulgent thoughts tend to be overshadowed by facts and figures. Instead, let your style guide all the choices you'll make in creating a kitchen plan.

Think of your favorite things. Turn to a favorite travel destination, artwork, or hobbies such as antiquing or gardening to make your kitchen your own, rather than a carbon copy of something you've seen. Books, magazines, and showrooms are great for ideas, but you need to personalize your home.

BELOW: **The desire for a panoramic view of a yard that often includes deer and wild turkeys inspired a wall of windows and more efficient, but fewer, base cabinets.**

OPPOSITE: **An arch above the pass-through between a kitchen and family room set the tone for a makeover of both rooms to create a unifying, pleasing whole.**

Look around. The kitchen often opens to a dining room, family room, or great-room. Visually connect the spaces by pulling in colors, textures, and design themes from the adjoining rooms.

Be selective. Make a list of colors, materials, and amenities you like, and then pare it down. Narrowing your choices doesn't limit your options; it helps you create a unified space.

Be realistic. Whether creating an entirely new space or revamping an old one, consider the kitchen's layout from the floor up. Work with a design professional to make the most of your kitchen space and integrate it with the rest of your home, particularly if remodeling means a change of floor plans

OPPOSITE: Inspiration came from the homeowner's grandmother's kitchen. Weathered brick composes a fire wall behind the professional-grade range. Vintage-look cabinets are stocked with modern-day amenities and conceal kitchen essentials.

BELOW: Open-shelf cabinets crafted from plywood and maple veneer were designed for aesthetic reasons but proved functional for ease of storage and accessibility to frequently used items. The open look also helps the small kitchen live larger.

explore your options

Every space has potential. Open your mind to the possibilities for an ideal floor plan within your existing kitchen. ››

>> The layout is critical to how much you'll enjoy being in your kitchen. Sure, you can fill it with gleaming cabinetry, granite counters, and exotic flooring, but what good will they be if you're constantly tripping over children, guests, the dog, or another cook? The floor plan that will work best for your kitchen will be based on three things: work triangles, zones, and the shape of your space.

kitchen layouts

LEFT: Eliminating a swinging door between the kitchen and butler's pantry improved traffic flow. The range is part of a U-shape work zone that also contains the refrigerator and prep sink, *not shown*. A tucked-away cleanup zone with a large sink, dishwasher, and cabinets for storing dishware is housed in the butler's pantry beyond.

BUILDING BLOCKS

The kitchen work triangle is formed by the refrigerator, the sink, and the cooktop or range. A line drawn from the center of the sink to the center of the refrigerator to the center of the cooktop, then back to the sink's center should measure no more than 26 feet. Active cooks may prefer 22 feet or less. In either case, each side of the triangle should measure at least 4 feet but no more than 9 feet.

Zones, also known as work centers, are concepts that complement work triangles. By planning zones and the triangle, you'll ensure that different functions, such as preparation, cooking, and cleanup, can be carried out without collisions. Certainly these chores are likely to occur within a triangle arrangement; other functions are placed outside

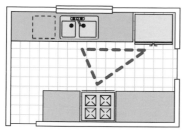

GALLEY KITCHEN

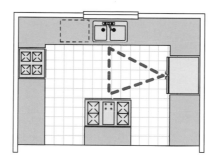

U-SHAPE WITH ISLAND

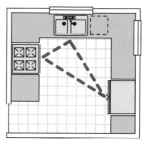

U-SHAPE KITCHEN

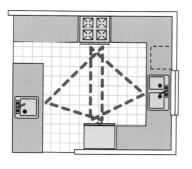

TWO-COOK KITCHEN

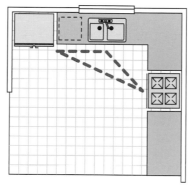

L-SHAPE KITCHEN

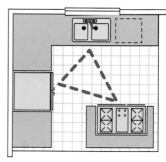

L-SHAPE WITH ISLAND

G-SHAPE KITCHEN

ONE-WALL KITCHEN

Consider these eight kitchen shapes as a place to start your planning. The work-triangle design within each can be flexible, so make adjustments to meet your needs.

it. A zone for unloading groceries, for example, requires a stretch of counter space near the refrigerator. A coffee zone with brewer, mugs, spoons, sugar, and cream could be near the sink (or have its own), and should be placed where family and guests can help themselves without crossing a cook's path.

Depending on the dimensions of your kitchen, one or more of several basic kitchen shapes will be most efficient and pleasing to you. The basic shapes are, however, just a starting point. Customize them: Put two shapes together or carve out a 90-degree corner for an angled stretch of counter—whatever you need to get a kitchen that works for you.

One-wall kitchens are an efficient use of small, open spaces, but they're not terribly efficient for the cook. They work best with the sink in the center, flanked by fridge and cooktop with 4 feet of counter between each pair. Place doors away from the one-wall shape to avoid foot-traffic hassles.

Galley kitchens are built between parallel walls, allowing the cook to move easily from one work area to another. Leave at least 4 feet between opposite counters; think about putting the sink and fridge on one wall with the cooktop centered between them on the opposite wall. If there are doorways at each end of the galley, foot traffic can cross the work triangle.

L-shape kitchens require two adjacent walls and are particularly efficient when work areas are kept close to the crook of the L. You'll save yourself extra steps by planning the workflow from fridge to sink to cooking, then to serving

ABOVE: New columns, built-ins, and an overhead beam offer a period-appropriate transition to this dining area. French doors create a wall of glass that opens onto the deck.

LEFT: Even a freshly remodeled kitchen can embrace new as well as old. The homeowner received this maple butcher block as a gift from a butcher for whom he had built a house. The homeowner kept the piece for 20 years and put it to use in this kitchen after realizing that the central island, which includes drawers for easy access to pots and pans, could use a little more work space.

OPPOSITE: Though shortened to open up the kitchen's entryway, this wall is more functional and attractive than before. It contains one of two pantries, electric-convection and microwave ovens, and storage spots for cookbooks and wine.

areas. Crossing foot traffic is rarely a problem in the L-shape kitchen.

L-shape-with-island kitchens make room for multiple cooks, snack bars, and increased storage. Typically they allow for in-kitchen family dining as well. The island also works as a visual divider.

U-shape kitchens usually place one workstation on each of three walls. The design possibilities are many and can be efficient for one cook, but you'll need at least an 8×8-foot kitchen. Small U shapes can be a tight squeeze for more than one cook.

U-shape-with-island kitchens solve the dilemma of making a big kitchen

efficient. You can work a sink or cooktop into the island, or even a special-function countertop, such as butcher block for chopping or marble for rolling out pastry. Allow 42 inches of aisle space on all sides of the island; 48 inches is better in a two-cook kitchen.

G-shape kitchens feature an island-type feature anchored to a line of cabinets. Cooktops or sinks work well situated on the peninsula, which can also function as a dining bar or buffet. The peninsula can be a room divider, allowing family and friends to hang out with the cook without crossing paths.

Two-cook kitchens call for work

zones or triangles that allow each cook to work without crossing the other's path. Two work triangles can, however, share a leg and are often anchored at the fridge. Multiple-cook arrangements may—but need not—include an extra prep sink, an additional stretch of countertop, or a small second refrigerator.

Designer Tip

Ovens are the least used element of a work triangle. You can gain cabinet space by locating ovens just outside the triangle.

big cooking

A large kitchen offers numerous design options because of its sheer size, but the elements must be arranged carefully to make the space both efficient and comfortable. Generally, a large kitchen should be divided into zones with distinct functions—cooking, eating, relaxing, and working—so that each feels intimate and cozy while remaining a part of the whole.

One of the best ways to accomplish this is with a center island. A cooktop or sink can be built into the island, along with ample counter space, so that the cook can interact with family members in the kitchen rather than face a blank wall. Islands concentrate food preparation, serving, and cleanup zones in one area so the cook doesn't waste time trudging back and forth across a large room with milk jugs, heads of lettuce, knives, cans, or bottles in hand.

A spacious kitchen often affords room to set up multiple, compact work

LEFT: Textural details—a stucco range hood, a bluestone-and-granite floor, and furniture-style pine cabinetry—give this sprawling kitchen warmth.

triangles to accommodate more than one cook at a time. For example, a second sink can be used for food prep or as a wet bar when entertaining.

OPPOSITE: This floor plan attests to how kitchens have evolved into multipurpose, multizone suites. More than half of the 33×19-foot space is devoted to noncooking functions, including an intimate seating area set in front of a fireplace, *not shown*, and a generous, informal eating area.

RIGHT: This spacious kitchen offers two complete work centers to accommodate side-by-side cooking. The 10-foot-long dining table in the adjoining eating area was custom-made from old heart pine to fit the room's generous proportions. Twelve can sit comfortably; it's an ideal space for casual entertaining.

small kitchens

If you live with a small kitchen, you may not be able to outfit it with a fireplace, sofa, art easel, and computer station, but you can have a highly efficient and attractive space.

What are your minimum kitchen needs? Think about a stove, sink, refrigerator, and food prep/cleanup area. Decide the minimum dimensions within which you can work, and then arrange all the necessities—including storage—in that space.

Think of ways to conserve space. Look for appliances that are available in small sizes ideal for a diminuitive kitchen. Some built-in dishwashers, for example, come in an 18-inch width. Another option to help with a tight fit is an under-the-sink model that takes advantage of often-wasted space.

Also consider whether you can take advantage of adjoining spaces. Can you combine your kitchen with an adjacent room to make a multipurpose cooking, dining, and family room? Perhaps you can open up a wall, or a half-wall, between your kitchen and the adjoining room to improve flow and increase the sense of space.

OPPOSITE: Though this new kitchen's layout essentially matches that of the old one, creamy white cabinets accentuated by stainless-steel appliances and limestone counters create a fresh new look and the illusion of more space.

ABOVE AND LEFT: A blend of natural materials and modern shapes, such as the curved peninsula, results in a kitchen that feels cozy and looks cool. Frosted-glass fronts installed in stock cabinets give the feel of transparent glass but are more forgiving of jumbled dishes and cluttered cups, particularly in a small kitchen.

unfitted

An idea from the 1980s is now a full-blown trend that's likely here to stay. The unfitted kitchen features freestanding, furniturelike cabinetry, often paired with handcrafted items or repurposed flea-market finds to create an eclectic, highly personal look. Unfitted kitchens employ a mix of colors and shapes and may incorporate work spaces of different heights and materials according to their functions. There may be a marble slab for pastry making, heat-resistant granite near the oven, and a butcher block for chopping and slicing. In an unfitted kitchen, pieces often can be approached from more than one direction, as opposed to in a built-in or fitted kitchen, where elements are attached to the walls all the way around the room.

Nothing has changed the nature of kitchen storage as much as the proliferation of cabinets modeled after furniture. This trend fits homeowners who want their open kitchen's floor plans to coordinate with adjacent living rooms, dining rooms, and family rooms.

Whether or not you plan to incorporate family heirlooms into your kitchen, shop for your new storage and workstation pieces as if you're shopping for furniture. Stylewise, look for details from past centuries: turned legs, bun feet, corbels, fretwork, carved inlays, arched valances, fluted moldings, and punched-tin inserts. For a truly unfitted look, buy from various sources, making the most of the diverse shapes, heights, colors, and finishes. Then scatter these acquisitions throughout the kitchen. For a less eclectic look, focus on a single standout piece.

Keep in mind that placing furniture within a kitchen's footprint differs from designing with standard cabinets—same height, same width, same finish—that run from wall to wall. An unfitted kitchen looks as if it evolved over the years, a single piece at a time.

OPPOSITE TOP: From rustic to refined, furniture-style cabinetry turns a kitchen into a warm, welcoming place for family and friends. Fine-furniture details—such as carved legs (these are salvaged bedposts) and a beaded-board base—make the kitchen island a standout.

OPPOSITE BOTTOM: This granite-top island is crafted in rich natural wood to counteract the light cream-color cabinetry. It includes a sink, a vegetable steamer, a trash compactor, deep drawers, and room for bar-height seating, all while maintaining a period presence.

BELOW: Custom cabinets outfitted with feet, molding, old-fashioned bin pulls, and white porcelain knobs combine with a table-legged island to create a room brimming with furniture style.

fitted

Fitted kitchens came into vogue in the 1950s, when matching, streamlined cabinets ran wall to wall. The design is somewhat formal and allows for maximum storage and counterspace. Fitted kitchens usually employ standard built-in cabinets, which are more economical than custom cabinets. With a bit of creativity, these cabinets can have warmth and personality and avoid the pitfall of seeming monotonous or institutional. Put glass fronts on some of the cabinets and light the interiors; use an interesting and functional countertop material; paint the cabinets a bright color; or hire a carpenter to customize one section—perhaps to build open shelving or a dresser for displaying a collection of favorite dishes.

LEFT: This fitted kitchen is warm and inviting thanks to natural hues and materials, including maple cabinetry, granite countertops, and a ceramic-tile backsplash.

ABOVE: Glass panels and colorful pottery imbue this cabinetry with extra personality and combat boxiness. Even in a fitted kitchen, consider a change of materials, such as the maple butcher-block slab that tops this island.

Even if space is at a premium, try to have an eating area in your kitchen. Party guests and family members seem to congregate there, and you'll have a place for them to sit. This can be accomplished with an island or in a space-saving built-in banquette or window seat. Round tables fit better into small spaces than rectangular or square ones. A small round table (about 4 feet in diameter) will seat four comfortably.

RIGHT: The most dramatic element in this tiny condominium kitchen—a curved, granite-top table spanning the window—is versatile, as well. At countertop height, it adds almost 6 feet of counter space for use as a work surface between meals or as a buffet.

BELOW: This area blurs the lines between the kitchen, family room, and dining room. For a quick bite, pull up a stool to the center island. For a more relaxed dinner, the dining room banquette adjoins the kitchen.

eat-in kitchen

ABOVE: This large kitchen island serves primarily as a breakfast bar, complemented by cheerful morning sunshine. The expansive surface also works as a food prep area when dishes are cleared.

LEFT: Banquettes are an attractive option for informal dining, because they conserve space without sacrificing comfort or style. This nook enjoys daily use—from family breakfasts to homework hour.

facelift

A kitchen that works well but looks dated or bland can benefit from an infusion of style. Facelifts include all nonstructural, cosmetic changes, such as repainting or papering the walls, resurfacing countertops, and/or replacing fixtures, flooring, and countertops.

Particularly if the cabinets are of good quality and provide sufficient storage, a facelift can be an ideal solution to instill new life in a kitchen with a case of the blahs.

In this kitchen, *right*, brown wooden cabinets and linoleum flooring were outdated, and poor lighting made the room feel cramped. Appliances had begun to deteriorate. On the plus side, the kitchen was a generous 400 square feet with quality cabinet construction and an efficient work area.

Because the cabinetry was well-made, it was left in place and revived with a coat of buttery yellow paint. New hardware completed the cabinetry transformation. The savings from keeping the cabinets allowed more money to go toward new surfaces and appliances.

Terra-cotta floor tiles lend old-world flavor and are a welcome replacement to the dated linoleum. Honed-granite countertops add warmth but in a dark contrast to the yellow cabinets. Window openings were expanded to bring in more light.

RIGHT: A butcher-block-top island replaced a small table that once occupied the center of this kitchen. The island provides more work space and a storage area underneath.

Get Happy. Make sure you are truly happy with the layout of your kitchen before you undertake the effort and expense of a kitchen facelift. Even though the savings are significant compared to a renovation or an addition, the costs for a facelift will still add up when you figure in paint, new hardware for each cabinet and drawer, fixtures, lights, flooring, and countertops. If your kitchen doesn't function well for your family, a fresh coat of paint won't help. Consider working with a design professional to determine how to make your budget address your most pressing kitchen remodeling needs.

renovate
same space

The average kitchen design remains functional and aesthetically pleasing for about 15 years. That means if you've recently moved into anything but a brand-new house or have been in your house for even a few years, you're probably itching for a change in your kitchen.

Maybe you want to reconfigure your appliances to do away with gridlock around the snack cabinet, microwave oven, or refrigerator. Maybe you've got a burn mark on your laminate countertop from that big pot of refried beans you set down on it, and the blemish has

inspired you to start anew. Maybe you simply want a new look. The allure of state-of-the-art appliances; newly available materials for cabinetry, flooring, and countertops; and the latest array of fresh, new colors is undeniable.

One way to design a new kitchen is to stay within the walls of your original kitchen but rearrange its elements. Maybe that's a matter of relocating the cabinetry, stove, sink, and refrigerator. Maybe it means adding or removing walls, or adding or enlarging windows and doors. Perhaps a wall can be made

into a half-wall to open up the kitchen to an adjacent living area, increasing the sense of space without completely moving any walls.

The layout of your kitchen is determined by where the four major elements—the sink, range, refrigerator, and dishwasher—are placed. The style of your kitchen can, but certainly doesn't have to, influence its layout. A similarly sized Craftsman-style kitchen and Mediterranean-style kitchen may each have the stove, sink, refrigerator, and dishwasher in the same spots, but they

may be housed quite differently, and the furnishings and materials used may differ. Very contemporary kitchens often feature banks of streamlined cabinets and are built with high-tech materials.

OPPOSITE: Removing a wall between the kitchen and breakfast area opened up this kitchen and made both spaces brighter because light from windows in the kitchen area can now filter into the breakfast nook.

ABOVE: New custom oak cabinets have a Mission look, appropriate for this 1915 home. Glass-front doors on some upper cabinets and a mix of knobs, latches, and bin-style pulls contribute to the period look.

Measure Twice, Cut Once.
If you must stay within the footprint of your current kitchen, there's an easy way to move around the major players until you get everything to your liking. Plot the shape of your room on graph paper. Sketch windows and doors where they exist or where you'd like them. Do the same for water pipes, electrical outlets, and heating and cooling vents. Make to-scale cutouts of the appliances you're planning to buy. Move them around your drawing. You might need to buy a smaller appliance or try a different configuration. Sketch in cabinetry and countertops.

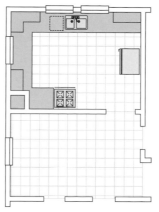

BEFORE

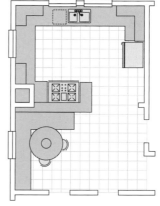

AFTER

borrow space

No matter the shape of your kitchen, increasing space—for eating, doing homework, or hanging out—and improving efficiency in meal preparation and cleanup are the primary considerations when redesigning the room.

A kitchen can be reshaped in many ways. You can stay within the exterior walls but rearrange the interior walls. Or annex all or part of an expendable powder room, bedroom, stairwell, or a rarely used formal dining area.

Perhaps you can knock down the wall that joins the kitchen to another living area and add an L-shape peninsula where the walls once stood.

It's possible to connect the kitchen visually and physically to the main living areas of the house and still keep the rooms separate enough that you don't have your dirty dishes on view. Consider opening up the kitchen to the second floor, or build a half-wall or pass-through so dishes and conversation can be passed back and forth between the rooms. Floor or wall cabinets can take the place of floor-to-ceiling walls, islands, or peninsulas as a way to reconfigure your kitchen and open it up.

Sometimes it takes only a few fixes to turn a clumsy kitchen into an efficient work triangle with ample counter and cabinet space. The original kitchen in this home, *left and opposite*, featured such a tight floor plan that the previous owners had placed the refrigerator far from the range and sink in a corner nook that was probably intended for a small kitchen table. This nook extended about 5 feet beyond the rest of the kitchen's north wall, creating an oddly shaped room and a zigzag circulation pattern.

The current owners eliminated side stairs and pushed out the rest of the north wall to form a square-shape room, doubling the counter and wall space. To create a conventional work triangle, they also rearranged appliances, placing the refrigerator where the range had

Designer Tip

New hardware is a fast way to spiff up old cabinets, but it doesn't always fit the holes your outdated knobs leave behind. Cover the existing holes with backplates and then drill new holes.

been and moving the range to the extended wall.

Storage was another priority. In addition to the extra cabinets that were installed when the kitchen was extended, the owners included a pantry-style cabinet next to the refrigerator. A hutch with glass inserts provides a stylish storage place near the stairs. There wasn't room for an island or peninsula with a break-

fast bar, so a bench and table were included where the refrigerator had been. The result is a new kitchen that's stylish and much more usable.

OPPOSITE: Cherry cabinetry with antique-style seeded glass in the upper panels lends Arts and Crafts-style warmth to the kitchen. The range is positioned along a wall that was expanded.

ABOVE: The enlarged kitchen allowed space to tuck in a cozy breakfast nook. A computer data port allows the table to double as a work area when meals are not being served.

add on

It seems almost everyone wants a bigger kitchen. People aren't just preparing food in kitchens anymore. Today's kitchens see all sorts of action: doing homework, painting, paying bills, surfing the Internet, chatting with a friend.

In new construction, nearly all kitchens are built with ample square footage and are designed to be eating and gathering spaces, with an open connection to at least one other room. But if you have an older house, space constraints can be a real problem.

Adding on—whether it's as simple as a bay window with banquette seating or as complex as a conservatory or an entire breakfast room—is undoubtedly the ideal (but, alas, most expensive) way to get your dream kitchen.

The simplest way to add on to your kitchen is to annex and close in an adjoining outdoor space, such as a breezeway or porch. Lacking that opportunity, you'll have to build out into your yard. (If you have a two-story house, and your nerves and budget can afford it, consider a two-story addition to gain a bathroom, office, or bedroom along with your expanded kitchen.)

If possible, design your kitchen addition so that it opens up to the outdoors. Any room benefits from fresh air and sunlight—a kitchen perhaps most of all. It's where you shuffle to first thing in the morning to wake up, greet the sun, and sip a cup of coffee or tea. In the evening, fresh air helps diffuse cooking odors. Putting on an addition also gives you the opportunity to add more windows, perhaps in the form of French doors that open onto a patio.

With access to the kitchen from the outdoors, countertops are easy to reach when you're lugging in groceries. It's a short trip from the garden for picking fresh vegetables and convenient to carry full plates of food to the patio or deck for an alfresco dinner.

You obviously want an addition to blend as seamlessly as possible with the rest of your house (and so do the neighbors). Here are a few pointers for getting the best results:

- **Take careful measurements.** Do a structural analysis and give weight to the findings. If you need to upgrade some of the home's underpinnings, spend the money before adding the finishes.
- **Choose materials** that combine with or mimic the home's original palette.

- **Consider in which direction it makes sense to expand.** Be sure to look into current building codes. You may need an exception or variance from the city before proceeding with your project. Even a little space can make a big difference. These tips will help you get the most from a small addition:
- **Play all the angles.** An angled addition can provide extra space and run parallel to your property line without looking bulky from the outside.
- **Turn the corners.** Wrap an addition around the kitchen.
- **Eliminate unneeded doorways** to make space for uninterrupted cabinets.
- **Create long sight lines.** Plan for unobstructed views from one end of the kitchen to the other.

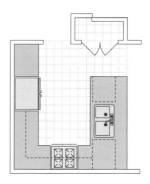

BEFORE

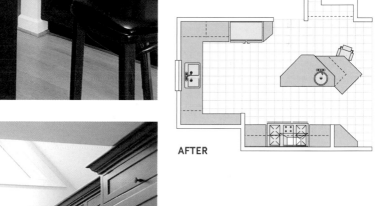

AFTER

OPPOSITE: A 6×10-foot bump-out improved traffic flow and created room for an island and professional-grade range.

ABOVE LEFT: The island offers a sink—convenient for food prep or when two cooks are working at the same time—as well as seating and storage.

LEFT: Adding on allowed for a vaulted ceiling and additional windows, bringing new light into the kitchen. Cherry cabinets and granite countertops flecked with metal add new style.

remodeling options

Certain criteria are common to most kitchen remodeling projects. They are:

- Get the most for your money.
- Make the space as efficient as possible.
- Include zones for each task and incorporate "point of use" storage.
- Facilitate easy maintenance.
- Create a kitchen that reflects your personality and desires.
- Maximize functionality and beauty.

Beyond that, every person and family has different priorities. One may want an aesthetically perfect space to blend seamlessly with the rest of the house—but may not cook much in it. Another may want the best appliances the budget allows for serious cooking and baking. Every remodeling pie gets divided and enjoyed very differently. Consequently, each remodeling job requires that compromises and choices be made so the homeowner gets the kitchen that best reflects who he or she is and how the room will be used.

ABOVE AND RIGHT: **Two very different kitchens can be built into the same space for the same money depending on the needs and desires of the people who will be cooking, eating, and living there. When making your own kitchen plan, make a list of your requirements, plan for those first, and then add luxuries if your budget will allow.**

TWO KITCHENS, TWO FAMILIES, SAME BUDGET

To show how one remodeling budget can be spent very differently depending on a family's needs and desires, we gave a hypothetical $35,000 to two hypothetical families to "spend" on a new kitchen that suited their needs, assuming they both started with the same outdated kitchen. Here's how their remodeling projects turned out.

FAMILY A:

(Father, mother, two young children)

Requirements:

- Lots of countertop area to make family meals
- Informal buffet serving area
- Large refrigerator
- Backyard view to watch children at play
- Kitchen open to family room
- Countertop seating for four
- Pantry storage
- Trash compactor
- Durable countertop surfaces
- Bulletin board for children's schedules and artwork
- Message center with phone
- Cookbook storage
- High-quality cabinets to make every inch of space hardworking

FAMILY B:

(Empty nesters with four grown children and grandchildren)

Requirements:

- Intimate seating for two
- Ample seating for when family comes to visit
- Upscale, easily operated appliances
- Gourmet coffeemaker
- Open feel for informal entertaining
- Glass doors to display collectibles
- Areas for two cooks to work at the same time
- Uncluttered, organized, sleek look
- Low maintenance
- Television with DVD/CD player
- Place to grow plants

budget: family A

CABINETRY: Custom raised panel $16,000.

COUNTERTOP: Granite with decorative edge $5,000.

APPLIANCES: Standard grade $3,800.

SINK, FAUCET, LIGHTS: Standard grade $3,000.

FLOORING, WALL FINISHES: Hardwood, paint $3,000.

CONSTRUCTION AND INSTALLATION:
Add pass-through opening $4,200.

TOTAL: $35,000

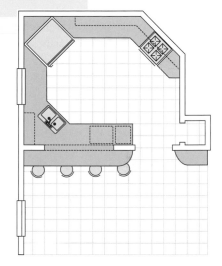

RIGHT: A peninsula in the family kitchen serves as both a dining area for casual meals and an informal buffet serving area for parties. It also provides additional seating for the adjacent family room. Tucked out of the way to the right of the peninsula is a small but hardworking message center to keep the family organized.

budget: family B

CABINETRY: Stock, with stained recessed panels $9,000.

COUNTERTOPS: Bevel-edge laminate $2,000.

APPLIANCES: Upgrade $9,500.

SINK, FAUCET, LIGHTS: Standard grade $3,000.

FLOORING, WALL FINISHES: Laminate, paint $2,000.

CONSTRUCTION AND INSTALLATION:
Remove wall, increase window size $9,500.

TOTAL: $35,000

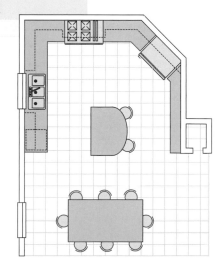

RIGHT: The homeowners—empty-nesters—needed two kinds of seating: cozy dining for just the two of them, and a generous table with lots of seating for when their grown children and grandchildren visit. In addition to seating room, the island provides ample food prep space to accomodate two cooks working in the kitchen at the same time.

budget sense

Part of a charming, 100-plus-year-old house, this formerly outdated kitchen would become heart-of-the-home to a professional chef/culinary writer, her husband, and five children between them. The cut-up floor plan was hardly up to the new demands. The homeowners ideally wanted to boost the efficiency of their kitchen with more counter space, more cabinet space, an entry closet to minimize clutter at the back door, more daylight, and a suite of up-to-date appliances—including a commercial range, a bigger refrigerator, a more efficient dishwasher, and a built-in microwave oven. They also wanted to include a baking area and breakfast table.

Their kitchen designer presented them with three options: minimal change for the least cost, moderate

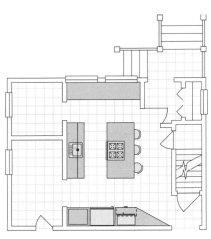

MINIMAL REMODELING

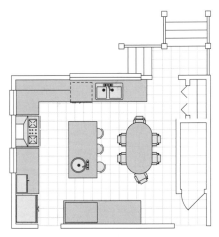

MODERATE REMODELING

BREAKFAST/
FAMILY ROOM

MUDROOM

KITCHEN

ALL-OUT REMODELING

change with moderate cost, and a high-end overhaul. Here's how the three plans looked:

Minimal remodeling floor plan: This plan proposed an island for dining and gathering space; included more counterspace and new efficient cabinetry; removed walls at the back door for a less-congested feel; and added a full-size refrigerator, a built-in microwave oven, and warming drawers. It did not include a commercial-type range because of the island location, did not add more daylight, and incorporated only minimal gathering space.

Moderate remodeling floor plan: This plan proposed removing all of the interior walls and adding a new window. In addition it added a vegetable sink and warming drawers to the island, a dining table, more daylight, and a 36-inch commercial-style range with hood—plus all of the improvements proposed in the minimal remodeling plan.

All-out remodeling floor plan: The plan that actually materialized turned the kitchen on its side, reshaping it from 12½×17½ feet to 19×13 feet. A butler's pantry was converted into a mudroom with a closet for a more convenient back entry. Alongside the new mudroom, a 14×16-foot breakfast/family room was added, with a peninsula dividing it from the kitchen work space. More than double its original size, the revamped multipurpose kitchen incorporated everything the homeowners wanted— and more.

family solutions

Though everyone needs a place to prepare meals and eat, the specific needs of families with children are very different from those of people without children at home or of serious cooks and entertainers. Consider the following floor plans, which illustrate how two families' needs were met in the same overall kitchen square footage.

Family one is composed of a husband and wife in their early 30s with three children, ages 2, 4, and 7. They are on a limited budget. Because the children are young, the kitchen needs to serve as not only a space for cooking and eating but also a place for family activity. Baking cookies, gardening, and antiquing are favorite adult hobbies.

The kitchen needs to serve primarily one cook, with room at the island for other activities. The homeowners want traditional cabinetry to go with their antiques, maybe maple with a honey-color stain because a light stain on a hard-grain wood is the most forgiving when hit with toys. Accessories should include a foldout pantry, recycling bins, tray storage for cookie sheets, and file drawers at the desk.

The appliances should be good-quality but not top-of-the-line gourmet equipment. The family needs a convection oven, a good-size freezer for garden produce, a compost chute, and a sink with double bowls. The countertops can be laminate. The floor needs to be more durable than wood but more forgiving than tile for the comfort and safety of the children—probably a laminate also.

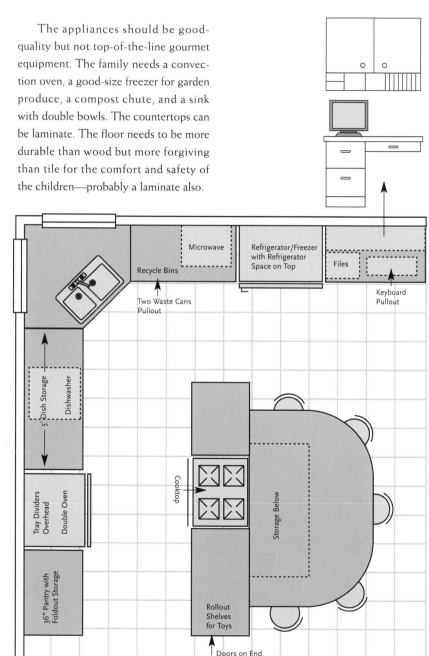

Family two is a couple in their 40s. They have a dog they love to pamper. They entertain friends often and enjoy cooking and eating elaborate gourmet meals paired with fine wine.

They are both serious cooks and need two distinct work triangles that won't interfere with each other. Though they would like an intimate dining area in the kitchen for themselves, they have an elegant dining room for use when they entertain.

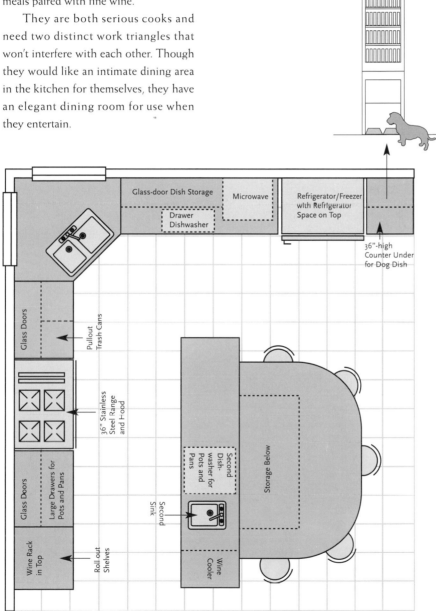

3

outfit your space

Choose materials and fixtures wisely so that your new kitchen will look great and perform beautifully. »

>> Learn about the newest features and options in appliances and materials before you go shopping. Choosing the right mix of products for your kitchen—and your budget—can help make your kitchen dreams a reality. A foray to a home improvement center or kitchen and bath store can be exciting and interesting—and mind-boggling.

cabinetry

Designer Tip

High-end cabinetry is worthy of its price tag not only for its appearance but also for its long-lasting quality and precision in every aspect, from construction to hardware. One example: Finished cabinet sides prevent moisture from compromising the integrity of the cabinet box.

To get the best cabinets for your budget, keep your work area compact and stick with standard sizes.

OPPOSITE: Casual yet hardworking, this kitchen features a mix of colors, materials, and freestanding pieces.

ABOVE: This freestanding hutch holds crystal and serving pieces. Beveled-glass doors reflect light from windows on the adjacent wall.

Probably more than any other element, cabinetry sets the look and feel of your kitchen. The right cabinet choices will help make the room efficient and easy to use. A kitchen remodeler once remarked that cabinets are "basically furniture you hang on your walls." Not surprisingly, their price tag reflects that interpretation.

According to the National Kitchen and Bath Association, nearly half—48 percent—of the average kitchen remodeling budget goes toward cabinets. If you choose custom-made cabinets, solid maple or oak, or exotic veneers, don't be surprised if those beauties consume an even bigger piece of the remodeling pie. Accessories, modifications, and unusual finishes increase the costs further.

Depending on how they're constructed and how much they can be customized, cabinets fall into three

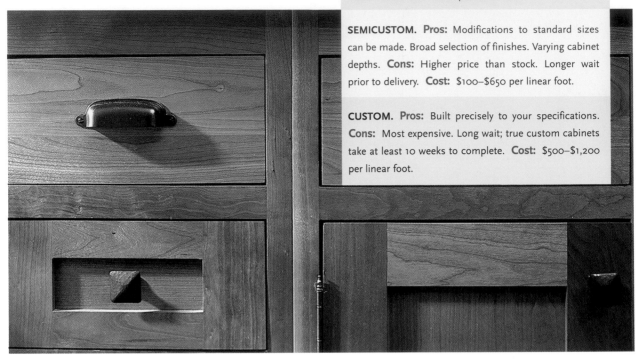

basic categories: stock, semicustom, and custom.

The category of a particular cabinet is not necessarily an indication of quality; fine cabinetry can be had in all three. Look for a blue-and-white "certified cabinet" seal from the Kitchen Cabinet Manufacturer's Association. It indicates that a manufactured cabinet has met certain guidelines for durable construction. A rundown of the types of cabinets currently available and the most common materials from which they're made follows.

STOCK CABINETS

Stock cabinets come in a great number of styles. Widths for stock cabinets run between 9 and 48 inches, increasing in 3-inch increments. Order through retailers, at home improvement and kitchen and bath centers, or from manufacturers' catalogs. Stock cabinets cost between $60 and $200 per linear foot.

Pros: Stock cabinets are usually the most economical choice. Because they are stored in manufacturers' warehouses, they are also readily available—usually within a week or so of being ordered.

Cons: Because the cabinets are already built—sitting in a warehouse waiting to be purchased—they don't come in special sizes. Filler strips can close gaps between a cabinet and an appliance or a wall, but that's pretty much the extent to which the cabinets can be customized. If only the "real thing"—solid wood—will do for you, it's unlikely you'll find what you're looking for in stock cabinets.

Make Good Choices. No single item affects the look, cost, and longevity of your kitchen as much as cabinetry. Buying the cheapest available is rarely the best choice. Drawers soon wobble on their substandard guide hardware or fall apart altogether, and inferior finishes wear away. Unless the cabinet surfaces are solid wood or wood veneer, painting or refinishing will be difficult or even impossible. When comparing cabinets, ask about construction details and look for these signs of lasting quality:

- Solid-wood face frames with doweled-and-glued joints, unless the cabinet is frameless. Mortise-and-tenon joinery is even better, but it's a custom-only feature.
- Solid-wood drawer fronts and door frames; solid or swell-veneered door panels.
- Solid-wood or plywood drawer sides at least 1/2-inch thick, with doweled or dovetailed joints (avoid stapled-and-glued joints).
- Self-closing drawer and tray glides able to bear at least 75–100 pounds each. Ball bearings are best. Full-extension glides increase storage space.
- Corner braces, plywood sides, and rear panels in the cabinet box.
- Adjustable shelves in wall cabinets.
- Pullout trays instead of fixed shelves in lower cabinets.
- Drawers and doors that open without any trace of wobbling or binding.
- Extended warranties and performance guarantees.

SEMICUSTOM CABINETS

These cabinets are built only after an order is final. They come in a wider range of styles, construction materials, and colors than stock cabinets. They can be amended easily with storage units and accessories, such as pullout bins and lazy Susans. Semicustom cabinets usually run between $100 and $650 per linear foot.

Pros: Because they are constructed after you've placed your order, modifications to standard cabinet sizes can be made. Semicustom cabinets offer a broad selection of finishes and varying cabinet depths that will give your kitchen a more personal look.

Cons: The primary disadvantage of semicustom cabinets is their higher price tag. They also may take a month or longer to be delivered after they're ordered, but when you're talking about a kitchen that should last up to 15 years, the wait shouldn't be a major issue.

CUSTOM CABINETS

These units are built, usually by a local cabinetmaker, from the material you choose (usually a hardwood, such as maple, cherry, walnut, or oak); in the

OPPOSITE: **Iron pulls on cherry cabinets suit this room's Craftsman theme and demonstrate the owners' careful attention to detail.**

ABOVE: **To showcase collectibles, install open shelving and glass-front cabinets. Plan for plenty of solid-door cabinets, as well, for items you don't want on display.**

size, shape, and configuration you choose; and with whatever finish you want. Custom cabinets usually cost $500 to $1,200 per linear foot.

Pros: The advantages are obvious: Within the limits of sound construction, your kitchen cabinets can look and function exactly the way you want. If you have an oddly shaped kitchen, a curved wall, or some other uniquely interesting aspect to your kitchen, it can be perfectly fitted with custom cabinets. You can also accommodate specialized storage needs. A long cabinet without interior partitions to hold cookie trays and roasting pans, for instance, can be created. If you use an experienced and artful cabinetmaker with a good reputation, the quality of your cabinets will be unsurpassed. Ask to see examples of past work and be sure to check references.

Cons: Far and away, the biggest downside of custom cabinets is their expense. And you can't be in a hurry to get cooking. True custom-made cabinets take at least 10 weeks—and often longer than that—to complete.

MATERIALS

Wood. Unless you're hiring a custom cabinetmaker, you may have a hard time finding solid-wood cabinets. That's OK; many high-quality units are made of plywood or particleboard. Drawer construction is an indication of quality: Look for metal glides with ball bearing rollers and dovetail assembly or screws and dowels (not staples and glue). Fully extended, the drawer should not wobble from side to side. Be sure the wood grain on doors matches the frame. To shave costs, order paint-grade units and do your own painting.

Laminate. Laminate cabinets are durable and easy to clean, and they come in an array of colors. High-pressure laminates perform best but are expensive. For strength, laminate should be applied to the backs of doors as well as the fronts.

ABOVE: A trio of stains—one for each tier—imbues these pale maple cabinets with a sheer wash of color. For an even softer look, choose tints close to that of the natural wood, with only subtle differences in tone and depth.

BELOW LEFT AND RIGHT: Complementary wood tones—maple and cherry veneers—add warmth to a clearly contemporary design.

hardware

If cabinets are furniture you happen to hang on your walls, hardware is jewelry for your well-dressed kitchen. Of course, hardware also has a very important function, and that should be your first consideration when purchasing it. Will that small, sleek, round brass knob work flawlessly on a floor-to-ceiling roll-out pantry loaded with canned goods? Probably not. But a sturdier handle would. For instance, one innovative homeowner fitted the drawers holding his heavy cookware with the kind of bowed handles found on hospital doors.

After determining which hardware will function well in your kitchen, you can move on to form. Certain types of knobs, hinges, and drawer pulls are associated with certain architectural styles or historical periods, but you don't have to be locked into those if you fancy something entirely different. Hardware is one way to personalize and decorate your kitchen.

Pricier models are usually the most sophisticated, including decorator-style pulls and hinges made of solid brass or nickel. Despite its name, hardware also comes in porcelain, ceramic, glass, plastic, and wood.

In the last five years, the biggest change on the hardware front has been the increased use of iron and weathered bronze. Several manufacturers, including Top Knob, Hafele, Amerok, and Belwith, have added these to their lines. Several firms also handmake pieces. The problem, of course, is cost. Purchasing five or six knobs for a bathroom at $25 a piece would be one thing, but the average kitchen requires between 30 and 60 pieces of hardware.

For a sleek, clean look, your cabinets can be fitted with invisible hardware. Doors can simply be opened on the hinges or can be fitted with spring-loaded hinges that pop the door open with a gentle push on the corner.

TOP: **Long, stainless-steel handles add architectural interest to European-style cabinet drawers and doors. Reeded-glass inserts in selected base-cabinet drawers break up what would have been a long expanse of wood.**

ABOVE: **If your cabinetry is sleek and contemporary, the hardware should concur. Go for a minimalist look that reflects your personal style.**

LEFT: **If you dream of earthy Tuscan villas and charming French farmhouses, select hardware with a rustic, weathered patina.**

countertops
and backsplashes

Two trends seem to be influencing countertop choices these days: a preference for natural or natural-looking materials, and a lack of inhibition about mixing and matching surfaces. Both trends open up exciting design possibilities, and manufacturers have responded with more choices than ever. Here's a look at the latest counter offerings.

LAMINATE

A laminate is a 1/16-inch-thick polymer layer bonded to 3/4-inch-thick plywood or particleboard. In the better varieties, the color runs all the way through the polymer sheet, helping to hide scratches and chips and eliminating the telltale brown line along the seam at the countertop edge.

Edges can be trimmed with beveled wood or metal inlays to create custom looks. A new twist is to fit laminate with edges made of solid-surfacing for corners that are rounded instead of angled. Postform laminate countertop sections are available with rolled front edges and backsplashes already attached. Laminate usually costs between $15 and $50 per linear foot installed.

Pros: Laminate is one of the least expensive countertop options. Experienced do-it-yourselfers may be able to install the surface themselves, further reducing costs. Most appealing, perhaps, is that laminate comes in a variety of colors, textures, and patterns, making it easy to match with other kitchen elements. Laminate resists grease and soap stains and is cleaned with soap and water.

Cons: Laminate is vulnerable to sharp knives and hot pans. Once damaged, the surface is hard to repair. In

BELOW: **Simply styled cabinetry made of natural-finish heartwood maple, which has more grain than hardrock maple, offsets the sleek stainless-steel counters and the blue backsplash tiles.**

some cases, prolonged exposure to water may dissolve gluelines and cause the subsurface to warp.

CERAMIC TILE

A ceramic tile is a piece of fired clay. The hotter the temperature and the longer it bakes, the harder and denser it becomes, with few air pockets for moisture to penetrate. Tile dense enough for countertops is termed vitreous. It can accept off-the-fire pots and pans without scorching, making it an excellent surface near a range, grill, or cooktop. Vitreous tile also resists moisture, so it can handle splashes and puddles around the sink.

Countertop tile may be glazed or unglazed. Glazing involves coating the tile surface with ground glass and pigments, then firing it again, making possible a wide range of colors and textures. Ceramic tile for countertops costs between $10 and $15 per linear foot.

Pros: The combination of incredible variety and great durability makes ceramic tile a worthy candidate for kitchen countertops. Sturdy ceramic tile comes in just about any size, shape, and color you can imagine. Creating patterns is ceramic tile's strong suit. You can use large field tiles and small accent tiles in contrasting colors to incorporate simple or elaborate bands, borders, and geometric shapes in your countertops.

Cons: Installing ceramic tile is a labor-intensive and potentially expensive venture. To reduce costs you can get a distinctive look by sprinkling a few expensive tiles into a field of economy tiles or reserve expensive tiles for the backsplash, where they won't suffer as much day-to-day abuse.

Ceramic tile is not a great surface for cutting, particularly if the glaze is a high gloss. The tile can dull knives, and knives can scratch tile. Manufacturers usually recommend against using high-gloss glazed tiles on countertops. Unglazed tiles come in different colors as well, though usually not bright hues.

Grout lines are the Achilles' heel of ceramic tile. Although the tile itself cleans up with a damp sponge, the grouted joints between tiles collect dirt and food particles and are prone to staining, particularly light-color grouts. Grout sealants are available.

STONE

In recent years, natural stone, particularly granite, has become the most coveted kitchen countertop surface. Tough, elegant, and virtually maintenance-free, granite is the choice of those who want the very best for their kitchen and are willing to pay for it. Granite starts at ¾ inch thick. Costs can vary greatly,

Quartz: A recent innovation in engineered surfaces is the use of quartz. One of the hardest of all natural substances, quartz imparts the durability and strength found in granite. Compressed with pigments and binders in large panels, it boasts an exceptional sparkle over a range of colors not found in other stone. Its properties, and the tools and techniques required for fabrication, are closer to those of granite than solid-surfacing panels. Cosentino's Silestone and Corian's Zodiaq are examples of engineered quartz. Installed cost runs $120–$200 per square foot.

depending on the quality, thickness, and availability of the variety you choose. Edge treatments, such as the popular bullnose look, can add to the cost. Marble and soapstone are other natural stone choices. Granite and marble usually run $75 to $200 per linear foot; soapstone, which is more porous, is available for $70 per square foot.

Pros: If you can get past the sticker shock, granite rewards your investment with years of faithful service. It cleans easily; endures water, hot pots, and sharp knives unscathed; and resists most stains. The ultrasmooth surface is wonderful for rolling out dough. Marble boasts similar qualities, is more porous than granite, and tends to stain more readily. Stone is as impervious to kitchen trends as it is to kitchen clatter—it never goes out of style. Granite, marble, and soapstone work with numerous looks, from traditional to contemporary.

Cons: The greatest prohibition is the price. Even if you can find salvaged pieces at a lower price, hauling and installing the heavy, hard-to-cut slabs is costly and definitely not a do-it-yourself endeavor. The other big drawback to stone countertops is lack of selection. You're limited to what nature creates on its own, and the colors and patterns tend to be subtle. Stone is porous and requires periodic sealing.

SOLID-SURFACING

More resistant to scratches than laminate and less likely to stain than marble, solid-surfacing is a ¼- to 1½-inch-thick sheet of synthetic material resembling stone that can be molded to fit any kitchen layout. Choices range from traditional stone patterns to a wide array of vivid solid colors, and special effects are possible by using inlays of contrasting colors to create borders or patterns. Solid-surfacing usually costs between $100 and $150 per linear foot installed. (Corian is the most well known, but

there are many makers, including Wilsonart and Avonite.)

Pros: Solid-surfacing offers more colors and patterns than natural stone and is lighter and easier to work with. A key feature allows your countertops and kitchen sink to be integrated, creating a seamless look that is design-friendly and aids cleanup. Solid surfacing can be routed, sandblasted, and even thermoformed into just the right shape.

Solid-surfacing is nonporous and

extremely durable. Because color runs all the way through the material, most minor damage can be repaired with an abrasive cleaner or a scouring pad, or with light sanding.

Cons: Knives and hot pots can scratch and burn the surface. Solid-surfacing also carries a high price tag. Purists may think of it as merely imitation stone.

STAINLESS STEEL

An up-and-comer on the counter charts, stainless steel offers an ultracontempo-

The pigmented finish is stain-resistant.

Cons: Concrete's appearance is not terribly versatile. It's most appropriate in very contemporary kitchens because it can look industrial. Also, concrete is not an easy material to replace.

BUTCHER BLOCK

Butcher block is made from hardwood strips—generally white oak, hard-rock maple, or beech—glued together. It comes in 1½- to 3-inch thicknesses and can be cut into any shape. Butcher block blends well with other countertop surfaces when installed atop an island or inset in a food preparation area. Its cost starts at about $50 per linear foot.

Pros: Butcher block imparts a sense of warmth in the kitchen and makes a great cutting surface, eliminating the need for a cutting board.

Cons: Moisture is not a friend to wood, so it can't be placed near wet areas. Finishing the wood may help protect it, but some finishes are not safe for food-contact surfaces.

OPPOSITE TOP: Topped with 3-inch-thick butcher block, a 4 1/2-foot-square island is the utilitarian and social centerpiece of this kitchen. The island conceals a large pullout trash bin.

OPPOSITE BOTTOM: Once sealed, copper countertops are very durable.

TOP: A butcher-block top of end-grain maple adjoins the work island's expanse of verde tropical granite, which was quarried in Brazil.

BOTTOM: Concrete countertops are an industrial touch for urban kitchens.

rary look and appeals to serious cooks who want surfaces that will match their commercial-style appliances. Stainless steel starts at about $65 per square foot (installed) for standard sizes. Custom sizes and cutouts for sinks are pricier.

Pros: Stainless steel is extremely durable and easy to clean, working well around stoves and sinks.

Cons: Stainless steel is somewhat priccy, and it does scratch. The clank of utensils on the surface can be irritating.

CONCRETE

Tough, reliable concrete keeps creeping further into the home. Now it's even finding favor as a countertop surface. Typically, concrete comes in large, seamless 1½-inch-thick sections or is poured in place. Concrete costs range from approximately $60–$130 per square foot.

Pros: Almost as durable as more-glamorous natural stone, concrete can be colored any shade. A sealer protects the color and makes the surface easy to clean.

flooring
and finishes

Floors take a lot of punishment in the kitchen. Foot traffic is heavy, and there's exposure to water, spills, and falling objects. You need a durable surface that's easy to clean yet stylish enough to anchor a high-visibility room.

CERAMIC TILE

With its range of shapes and sizes, tile offers texture, durability, and potential for patterns. Large formats, such as 12×12, 16×16, and 24×24 inches, are popular. They reduce the number of grout lines and the number of tiles to be installed.

Ceramic tiles are available unglazed or with a glaze that is fired onto the tile body. Fired glazes are extremely hard, but the chemical composition of a glaze and the amount of firing it receives determine whether the finished surface will be delicate, tough, or somewhere in between. Ceramic tile usually runs between $3 and $12 per square foot.

Pros: Its resistance to moisture and stains makes it an excellent choice. Ceramic tile is durable. In addition, you can match your flooring to countertops and backsplashes.

Cons: Ceramic tile is hard and can be cold. Several companies offer electric heat tape that can be installed on the subflooring before the tile is set.

LAMINATE

Plastic laminate features a decorative image—most commonly wood grain—printed on one or more thin sheets of paper or other fibrous material. For durability, the decorative layer is impregnated

RIGHT: Antique Provençal terra-cotta floor tiles installed in a herringbone pattern are warmed from beneath by hot-water coils in this Mediterreanean-inspired kitchen.

with a plastic or resin, such as melamine, subjected to high pressure, and bonded to a rigid core, resulting in a plank that's usually $5/16$ inch thick. A backing of kraft paper, resin-impregnated paper, or foil prevents warping. Laminate flooring costs between $4 and $11 a square foot.

Pros: Virtually stainproof, today's laminates are easy to clean, never fade, and never need waxing. A factory coating of aluminum oxide helps many floors resist damage from high heels, animal paws, and dropped dishes. A laminate floor simply requires damp mopping.

Cons: Long-term performance is yet to be proved. The material can sound hollow when walked on, though some manufacturers offer underlayments to help deaden the sound and vibration.

Laminate flooring is not impervious to wear. It will scratch and dent. Laminates are generally not recommended for use in high-moisture areas.

VINYL

Vinyl or resilient flooring is valued for its low price, low maintenance, durability, and array of colors, patterns, and styles. Vinyl is available in two categories: rotogravure and inlaid.

Rotogravure vinyl features a knobby texture, pattern, and color printed on the finished side. Inlaid vinyl's pattern and color run through the thickness of the material, improving durability. The wear layer on rotogravure vinyl is 10 to 15 mm thick; high-quality inlaid vinyl has a 25- to 30-mm-thick wear layer.

Vinyl comes in 6- and 12-foot-wide sheets and in various size tiles. Vinyl tile comes with either a dry back that is laid in adhesive or a peel-and-stick backing. Vinyl flooring costs between $1 and $5 per square foot.

A Terra-Cotta Caveat. Soft clay terra-cotta tiles, such as red clay Mexican tiles, look great but will chip fairly easily. Very often, these tiles are hand-made and are chipped even before they are glazed. The surface also tends to wear down in traffic lanes. It's important to be aware of this ahead of time and accept the flaws as inherent to the style of the tile. Other red clay tiles have very clean, sophisticated glazing. But beware: They still don't wear as well as ceramic tiles.

Pros: Vinyl has a low square-foot cost and is easy to maintain. Its resilience means a dropped glass has a good chance of bouncing rather than breaking, and vinyl is fairly comfortable to stand on.

Sheet vinyl has few or no seams, making cleaning a breeze. If there is damage to a vinyl tile, just that tile can be replaced.

Cons: Vinyl is subject to damage from burns, high-heel shoes, and large appliances. The seams on vinyl tiles can trap dirt and allow spills to filter between tiles, loosening them and damaging the subfloor. Less-expensive grades may fade and discolor quickly.

STONE

Today's stone tiles—boulders sliced into thin tiles and polished—aren't much different from those used centuries ago. Stone tiles are cut into a variety of shapes and sizes, though most come as 12-inch squares. Some feature a special surface treatment, such as a polished finish.

The most commonly used stones for tiles include granite, marble, and slate. Manufactured stone, made from hard quartz, is a new type of stone tile. Countertop materials Silestone and Zodiaq are both available in thinner pieces for the floor. Marble or granite runs $5 to $30 or more per square foot; slate can be had for much less, at $3 to $12 a square foot.

Pros: Some stone tiles, such as granite, are virtually indestructible. Engineered quartz floors are extremely dense and nonporous and are much more difficult to break than real stone. The look of a stone floor is classic and elegant.

Cons: Stone requires periodic sealing to guard against moisture absorption. Its weight prohibits it from being a do-it-yourself project. It's very expensive.

HARDWOOD

Wood flooring generally consists of solid, one-piece boards of hardwood. Fear of water damage steers some away from wood, but today's acrylic and urethane finishes offer great protection.

Red oak is the most common hardwood flooring, though other woods are gaining popularity. More expensive varieties include maple, ash, birch, cherry, hickory, and walnut. Imported hardwoods, such as Brazilian cherry, mahogany, and teak, also are gaining interest. Hardwood floors generally cost between $6 and $14 per square foot.

Pros: Wood flooring is warm and attractive and adds character. Hardwood floors last longer than vinyl and can be refinished several times, or even restained to change their appearance.

Cons: A wood floor in a kitchen is likely to have water, juice, or coffee dumped on it or to have a leaky appliance spew water across it. Moisture damages wood; the shrinking and swelling (as much as ⅜ inch) can pull tongues out of grooves, compromising the integrity of the floor and causing it to buckle or warp.

CONCRETE

Concrete is gaining a foothold in the kitchen. Although it can be dyed in the mixing process, concrete's greatest color potential comes after it has been poured. Once smooth, the wet concrete receives a powdered color hardener, which is mixed in with a trowel. This method can incorporate any color or several shades of pigment in varying amounts for a swirly, mottled effect. Basic concrete flooring costs about $4 to $10 per square foot, including installation.

Pros: Easy to clean, concrete can mimic natural stone at a lower cost and can be dyed any color. It's extremely durable and easy to maintain; sealing has to be done only every six to eight years.

Cons: Concrete is hard, can be uncomfortable to stand on, and spells destruction for dropped dishes.

LINOLEUM

Patented in 1863, linoleum—not to be confused with vinyl—is better than ever. To make linoleum, natural materials,

including linseed oil, resin, cork, limestone, and wood flour, are fixed with pigments; rolled onto a jute backing; and dried. As the linseed oil oxidizes, the linoleum becomes harder than vinyl. Linoleum costs about $45 or more per square yard, including installation.

Pros: Linoleum is made of natural components. It's far more durable than vinyl, lasting up to 40 years, and doesn't show scuffs and scratches. Linoleum cleans up easily with a damp mop.

Cons: Linoleum tiles have seam lines, which can trap dirt and moisture, and linoleum requires an occasional waxing—usually with water-based, self-polishing wax—to retain its shine. It can be noisy when walked on.

CORK

The material for cork tiles—usually 12×12 inches—comes from the renewable bark of cork oak trees. Cork tiles have a mottled grain similar to burled hardwood and come in a variety of stains. Cork tiles cost between $4 and $9 per square foot; planks cost between $7

flooring options

CERAMIC TILE. Pros: Moisture- and stain-resistant. Durable. **Cons:** Hard. Cold. Grout difficult to clean. **Cost:** $3–$12 per square foot.

LAMINATE. Pros: Virtually stainproof. Easy to clean. Won't fade. **Cons:** Prone to scratches and dents. Sounds hollow when walked on. Not recommended for high-moisture areas. **Cost:** $4–$11 per square foot.

VINYL. Pros: Inexpensive. Easy to maintain. Resilient. Easy to clean. **Cons:** Subject to damage from burns and high heels. Seams can trap dirt. Inexpensive grades can fade quickly. **Cost:** $1–$5 per square foot.

STONE. Pros: Some types are virtually indestructible. **Cons:** Requires periodic sealing. Expensive. Requires professional installation. **Cost:** $5–$30 or more per square foot for marble or granite. Slate can be $3–$12 per square foot.

HARDWOOD. Pros: Can be refinished several times. Lasts longer than vinyl. **Cons:** Subject to water damage. **Cost:** $6–$14 per square foot.

CONCRETE. Pros: Durable. Easy to maintain and easy to clean. **Cons:** Hard. **Cost:** $4–$10 per square foot installed.

LINOLEUM. Pros: Durable. Won't show scratches. Easy to clean. **Cons:** Requires occasional polishing. Seams can trap dirt and moisture. **Cost:** $45 or more per square yard installed.

CORK. Pros: Moisture-resistant. Easy to maintain. Resilient. Easy to clean. **Cons:** Urethane finish must be sanded off and reapplied every few years. **Cost:** $4–$9 per square foot.

and $8. Installation costs $1 to $4 per square foot.

Pros: Cushiony cork is a noiseless, comfortable, moisture- and temperature-resistant flooring. It can last for decades and resists damage from dropped items and even high heels. Regular maintenance is simply sweeping and mopping.

Cons: The urethane finish on cork needs to be maintained to ensure easy everyday care. Every few years, the old finish needs to be sanded and new urethane applied.

OPPOSITE: **Cork floors create a natural feeling and are comfortable underfoot.**

LEFT: **Arizona flagstone outfits this kitchen floor with showstopping shape. A hydronic heating system (hot water circulating in tubes buried under the stones) radiates welcome warmth.**

sinks

Garbage disposals. Among the less-glamorous aspects of your kitchen, these appliances sure are handy. They come in varying capacities and motor sizes, but perhaps one of the most interesting (and quiet) developments in the last few years is the HydroMaid water-powered disposal.

It has no motor and no parts that can corrode, and takes up a lot less space under the sink than a traditional disposal. You operate it by turning on a water valve mounted on the counter or the sink, or even hidden inside the cabinet. As long as you have at least 40 pounds of water pressure, the water operates an internal piston that moves the five stainless blades that grind the food waste into fine particles. This disposal can be used even with a septic system.

ABOVE LEFT: This stainless-steel sink complements appliances and offers a neutral balance to some of the stronger elements in a black, white, and orange-red kitchen. The smaller bowl offers a spot to tuck in the faucet without the need for additional counter space.

ABOVE TOP RIGHT: Grooves in the countertop channel water back into this wide and deep farmhouse-style sink. A walnut strip defines the sink's apron front and catches dribbles.

ABOVE BOTTOM RIGHT: This two-bowl, undermounted sink allows a modern stainless-steel basin to be incorporated into an old-fashioned country decor.

Shopping for a kitchen sink involves making numerous choices about material, installation method, size, cost, color, and bowl configuration. But don't despair. Here's what you need to know about your kitchen sink.

Although a standard sink is traditionally 6 to 8 inches deep, 10- to 12-inch-deep sinks are gaining in popularity thanks to their ability to hold big pots and lots of dishes, and to keep water from splashing out. Whatever you choose, rest assured that there's a material out there to suit your kitchen decor, size requirements, maintenance concerns, and budget.

INSTALLATION

Once you've chosen the material for your kitchen sink (see Kitchen Sink Options, *right*), you can decide how to install it.

Self-rimming: The easiest and most common method sets the edge of the sink on top of the counter. The bowl is dropped into a hole in the countertop, the plumbing is hooked up, and the edge is sealed. The main drawback is that the edge of the raised sink acts as a barrier when you try to sweep crumbs into the basin, and food particles can get stuck in the seam.

Tile-in: This method is an option only when your countertop is ceramic tile. The tiles climb right up to the edge of the sink and there is no—or very little—step-down or step-up. Apron-front sinks work well with this method because of their wide walls.

Undermount: Popular with solid-surfacing or stone countertops, undermount installation creates a sleek, unbroken line from counter to basin. The edge of the sink rests underneath the counter, a look right at home in a contemporary kitchen. Brushing scraps into the sink is a cinch. This installation

method can increase labor costs because the countertop must be customized to suit your sink's size and shape.

Integral: Integral sinks offer an even smoother line between the countertop and sink than undermount installation. An integral sink and countertop are one piece; there's no differentiation between the two. In the past, integral sinks have been made only of solid-surfacing. However, some manufacturers now feature stainless steel as an integral option. Natural stone also is available but with a weighty price tag.

CONFIGURATION

You no longer have to settle for the same old double-bowl sink. The options have multiplied—as has the number of basins and accessories.

Single-basin: Small kitchens might require a sink with just one bowl. A single-basin sink also makes an ideal second sink in a large kitchen with a dedicated food-prep area. Today these sinks are wider and deeper than ever and can handle large pots and cutting boards with ease. Sinkmakers offer models in numerous shapes, including rectangles,

Making a Match. Your sink and faucet should work as a team. When choosing mates, consider these points:

The ideal kitchen faucet is tall enough to fill pots and can rinse all corners of your sink. One option is a faucet with a retractable head that allows you to spray water where you want it.

To avoid splashes, make sure the faucet's height and the sink's depth are compatible. Also check the faucet's reach: Water should flow to one side of the sink's center, but not toward the back. Extra-deep kitchen sinks and those with more than one basin often require special faucets to guarantee the appropriate height and reach.

Wall-mount faucets offer the most flexibility when it comes to height. Because widespread and single-lever models can be deck-mounted, they can be positioned behind or beside sinks.

If you need to replace a center-set faucet, consider a mini-widespread version. It looks like a separate spout and handles but will fit existing center-set holes.

BELOW: Dual sinks offer flexibility for a two-cook kitchen. This island contains a small copper sink, whereas the cleanup zone consists of a large farmhouse-style sink.

OPPOSITE TOP: A matching copper sink and faucet is visually appealing as well as functional—the faucet contains a chilled water purifier and is handy for washing vegetables.

ovals, circles, and combinations, so you can choose a sink that adds both visual interest and convenience.

Double-basin: The standard two-bowl sink has received a makeover. Curved bowls add eye appeal, and configurations with one large and one small bowl allow the convenience of two bowls with the customized size most homeowners crave. Many two-basin sinks also come with one shallower side, which works well for rinsing vegetables or draining pasta. Some companies call these "1½-basin" sinks.

Triple-basin: If you've got the space, a triple-bowl sink is a desirable indulgence. Two large basins—ideal for stacking dirty dishes—often flank one small, shallow bowl, which is good for cleaning veggies. Sink manufacturers usually offer accessories, such as colanders, cutting boards, sink grids, and drainers, that snug into the shallow basin for easy food preparation. Some of these sprawling sinks have two basins and an extra stretch of ribbed drainboard, which is perfect for air-drying clean dishes.

LEFT: Consider material options. A slate farmhouse sink has the look of soapstone without the price. A weekly application of mineral oil maintains the deep black finish.

faucets

Today's faucets are more stylish and dependable than ever before. Longer, taller spouts—and pullout or retractable faucets—assist you in doing a variety of kitchen tasks more quickly and easily, including filling pasta pots or rinsing out the sink.

Solid-brass, die-cast innards are a sign of a high-quality faucet, but they often come with a hefty price tag—anywhere from $250 to $500 or more. Beware of faucets with plastic shells or handles. The price may be right, but their durability and resistance to scratching are likely to disappoint.

There are four basic types of kitchen faucets: ceramic disk, cartridge, ball, and compression.

Single-handle, disk-type faucets operate a pair of ceramic disks that slide over each other to regulate water flow and temperature. These faucets are typically the most durable and trouble-free. The disks and mixing chamber are located in a large cylinder that is held in place with screws.

Cartridge-type faucets come in both single- and double-handle configurations. Designed for ease of repair, the flow mechanisms are housed within a cartridge that can be replaced when leaks occur.

Single-handle, ball-type faucets have a rotating ball inside the faucet that moves over water inlet holes and permits water to flow, regulates the flow of hot

and cold water, and shuts off the water all together.

Compression-type faucets were common in households in the early 1900s. Each of two handles turns a large screw, also called a stem, inside the faucet. The stem has a washer on one end that is positioned over a hole through which the water flows. When screwed down tight, the washer fills the hole and blocks the flow of water.

As a safety precaution, some faucet models include antiscald controls that prevent the flow of water in excess of a preset temperature, usually 110 degrees. Antiscald devices can also be purchased and installed on existing faucets.

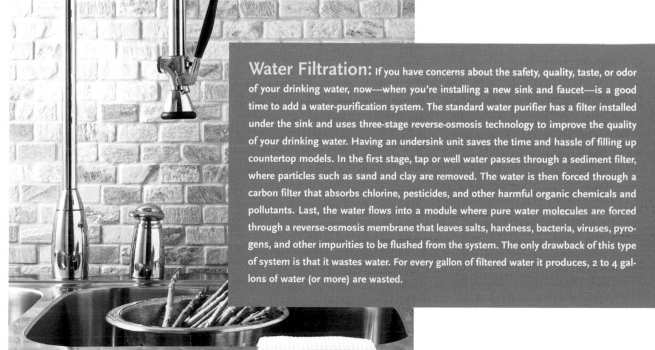

OPPOSITE: A gooseneck faucet with old-fashioned hot-cold connections makes filling deep pots easy.

ABOVE: This old-fashioned-look faucet and granite countertop are fitting choices for a farmhouse built in the late 1800s.

LEFT: A large arc and long hose length let you fill vases on the counter while veggies are draining in the sink.

Water Filtration: If you have concerns about the safety, quality, taste, or odor of your drinking water, now—when you're installing a new sink and faucet—is a good time to add a water-purification system. The standard water purifier has a filter installed under the sink and uses three-stage reverse-osmosis technology to improve the quality of your drinking water. Having an undersink unit saves the time and hassle of filling up countertop models. In the first stage, tap or well water passes through a sediment filter, where particles such as sand and clay are removed. The water is then forced through a carbon filter that absorbs chlorine, pesticides, and other harmful organic chemicals and pollutants. Last, the water flows into a module where pure water molecules are forced through a reverse-osmosis membrane that leaves salts, hardness, bacteria, viruses, pyrogens, and other impurities to be flushed from the system. The only drawback of this type of system is that it wastes water. For every gallon of filtered water it produces, 2 to 4 gallons of water (or more) are wasted.

cooktops,
ranges, and ovens

The symbolic hearth at the heart of the home is a major purchase. You can have an all-in-one range or a separate cooktop and wall oven; a standard 30-inch unit, or a gleaming, 60-inch professional-style range. And that's just the beginning. Here are some things to consider when choosing cooking appliances.

GAS OR ELECTRIC

Many cooks prefer the greater control and visual evidence of heat levels that gas burners offer. Gas also can be turned on and off instantly, and it's economical. Other cooks feel electric cooking is cleaner and easier.

If you choose gas, traditional burner grates can be removed easily for cleaning. Sealed-design gas burners prevent spills from seeping beneath them. On electric ranges, coil elements accommodate almost any cookware; glass-ceramic electric cooktops with radiant electric elements sealed beneath the surfaces are sleek-looking and easy to clean.

Compare the benefits of both types of cooking and decide which best meets your needs. Or look for a dual-fuel range model that combines a gas cooktop with an electric oven.

CONVECTION OR THERMAL

Convection cooking is now available as an alternative to thermal cooking in both gas and electric ranges. Thermal ovens use heat elements to roast, bake, and broil, whereas convection ovens use fans to circulate heated air around food for faster, more even cooking. Convection cooking produces crustier breads, juicier roasts, and multiple racks of cookies at one time.

RANGE SIZE

Range dimensions vary slightly; measure the space you have before you shop. The standard freestanding range is

ABOVE: In a vintage kitchen, a commercial-grade range is an acceptable concession to modern living. Here, a second oven was positioned just around the corner from the range.

OPPOSITE: This copper-plated exhaust hood creates a dramatic focal point, stretching nearly 20 feet overhead. Ventilation units must meet the minimum requirements for your range.

Double Ovens: Double ovens give frequent bakers and entertainers room to cook sumptuous holiday feasts or bake party-size batches of cheese puffs or cookies. Many new wall ovens are available with a convection option. With a double oven, you can cook food consistently at three or four rack positions and at different temperatures at the same time, and the smells from your roast won't contaminate your cake.

30 inches wide; restaurant-style models are available in 36-, 48-, and 60-inch widths. Remember cabinet depth: Flush cabinet installation offers a built-in look.

RANGE FEATURES

Easy-cleaning features: Self-cleaning ovens use a high-temperature cycle to burn food spills into a fine ash that is easy to wipe away. Continuous cleaning ovens have textured walls to absorb and burn spatters. Cooktops are made in a variety of smooth surfaces for quick cleanup. Electronic controls have a flat surface with no knobs to wipe around.

Safety features: Range and cooktop control locks protect children. Hot-surface indicators are useful for anyone who nears the stove.

Convenience features: Intuitive electronic controls are logical and have easy-to-read graphics. Some ranges offer one-touch controls preset to common cooking temperatures. Delayed and timed baking cycles allow the cooking process to start and stop even when you're out.

Performance features: Look for cooktops with a mix of outputs: high-Btu power for boiling and sautéing, and a simmer setting for cooking sauces and melting chocolate. (Btu stands for British thermal unit, a measure of heat energy.) Variable-temperature broiling lets you select the ideal temperature for anything from thick steaks to delicate fish.

DURABILITY

Ranges endure a lot of wear and tear over their 10- to 15-year life spans, so look for heavy-duty oven racks that support roasts and large casseroles,

porcelain broiler pans, and durable and dishwasher-safe grids. Expect at least a one-year warranty, five years on electronics and heating elements.

VENTILATION UNITS

You won't enjoy cooking one bit if you can't stand to be in your kitchen because of the heat or if you're chased out of the house by residual cooking smells. The solution to both of these concerns is a proper ventilation unit.

There are two types of ventilation systems. An updraft range hood hangs over the cooktop and sucks up steam and odors, venting them outside. A downdraft system is usually a vent built into the back of a cooktop. It's not as obtrusive as an updraft system, but it's usually not as effective, because it simply filters and recirculates the air rather than getting rid of it.

The size and power of your ventilation system will be determined by the kind of cooktop you have. Most residential kitchen ventilation units move

Designer Tip

If you're trying to restore your kitchen to a particular historical period and haven't found the perfect restored stove, a few appliance makers are turning out ranges that have modern conveniences packaged in period looks. Heartland offers the 1930s-style Legacy Series; the Classic Collection fits into Victorian and early-20th-century schemes. And a third line, Metro, features the look of commercial stainless steel with a bit of whimsy, such as a perfectly half-round oven window.

OPPOSITE: A stove, particularly one featuring additional counter-level work space, is best positioned near the main kitchen sink.

ABOVE: Tuck a microwave oven into its own space-saving cabinet cubby.

RIGHT: Eliminate the need for a view-blocking hood above the island by installing a downdraft exhaust system.

about 300 cubic feet of air or less per minute. That's fine for a standard four-burner electric or gas range or countertop unit. But commercial and pro-style ranges and burner units require larger ventilation units that can handle more heat and steam. Most of the commercial-style ranges generate between 15,000 and 16,000 Btus of heat. With even four burners on, that's the same 64,000 Btus that a small furnace puts out.

The ventilation requirement for commercial-style ranges is 300 cubic feet of air movement per running foot of cooking unit per minute. That means a 30-inch stove needs 750 cubic feet of air per minute. A 48-inch unit requires 1,200 cubic feet. Most of the ventilation units in that range cost more than $1,000.

COMMERCIAL-STYLE RANGES

If you cook a lot you're probably thinking about upgrading your 30-inch residential range to something with more power, features, and finesse.

A cautionary note: True commercial ranges, the kind that gleam in the galleys of five-star restaurants, are very costly. Some have price tags in the five-figure range, meaning you could easily blow your entire kitchen remodeling budget on just one item. Add to that the package of required accessories, including the high-capacity vent. You also have to accommodate the side and rear clearances these uninsulated fireboxes require. And after all that, you won't even have some key convenience features, such as a self-cleaning oven, built-in broiler, or electronic ignition.

In short, unless you have a mansion and a personal chef, you're probably better off with a "pro-style" range that combines much of the power, precision, and features of a commercial appliance in a user-friendly, flexible, easy-to-install package. And at approximately half the price of their industrial-weight counterparts, pro-style ranges leave some cash in your remodeling budget.

A pro-style range often features high-capacity and simmer burners, a grill or griddle, continuous grates, and a convection oven in a compact unit that fits flush into standard 24-inch-deep residential cabinetry. Most models also feature user-friendly conveniences such as self-cleaning ovens, built-in broilers, electronic controls, and pilotless ignition. They cost between $4,000 and $9,000—so the first question you have to answer is this: Do they fit the way you want to cook?

BURNER PERFORMANCE

Different manufacturers take different approaches to delivering professional-style performance. Many pro-style ranges have burners that generate up to 15,000 Btus, compared to the 10,000-Btu maximum of most residential ranges. These burners can boil liquids faster and sear meats more quickly. Thanks to their larger flame area, they also tend to heat more evenly. To distribute the heat, some manufacturers use a star-shape burner, others a dual-ring configuration.

Most residential ranges produce a minimum of 1,000 Btus. Some commercial-grade simmer burners can be turned down to produce half that much heat or even

less for delicate culinary jobs, such as melting chocolate. Dual-ring burners accomplish this feat by shutting off the outer burner ring; star-shape burners simply reduce the flame size or cycle on and off.

You'll find another classification for burners: sealed versus open. Sealed burners keep spills confined to the stovetop for easy cleanup. Open burners have drip trays that slide out for cleaning. Proponents of open burners claim they heat faster and adjust more precisely because of greater air supply to the burner flame. Others appreciate the convenience of sealed burners.

Pro-style ranges offer various cooktop configurations. Most 36-inch-wide ranges have room for six burners, but if four are plenty, you can usually equip the cooktop's middle section with a griddle or grill.

OVENS

Precise heat control on pro-style models is handled by thermostats that keep ovens to within 10 degrees of their setting for near-perfect baking. Because electric ovens maintain a somewhat steadier temperature than gas units, some stoves are dual-fuel, offering the speed and precision of gas burners with the more even heat of an electric oven. These units typically cost about 20 percent more than their all-gas counterparts. Some upscale 30-inch residential ranges also offer this option.

Virtually all pro-style ranges feature convection ovens. There are differences here too. All models feature a fan mounted in the rear panel, but American-style convection ovens circulate heat from the lower element, whereas European-style, or "true convection" systems, employ a third element that surrounds the fan, so the air is heated just prior to recirculation. The advantage, say proponents of the European system, is more even heat and less mixing of flavors when cooking more than one type of food at a time.

OPPOSITE: **Outfitted for serious cooking, this alcove houses a six-burner range with elevated griddle, regular ovens below, and an indoor grill on the adjacent countertop.**

ABOVE: **Pro-style ranges are not limited to stainless steel, as this striking blue range clearly illustrates. Coordinating cabinets are paired with the 48-inch range to visually expand the cooking area and the jolt of color.**

dishwashers

Dirty dishes can ruin a great meal. So how do you know that a dishwasher won't let you down? With dishwasher prices ranging from $200 to more than $1,500, it's vital to know which features you really need. Consider these characteristics and amenities as you shop.

SIZE AND TYPE

Measure the space for the new dishwasher and take the dimensions to the dealer. You can choose between built-in, portable, full-size, and compact models.

NOISE LEVELS

If family activities and conversations take place in or near the kitchen, a noisy dishwasher is irritating. The best way to reduce sound is to add or improve insulation around the washing tub, door, toe panel, and access panels. Some models offer extra-quiet motors and vibration-absorbing materials, but you will pay more for those features.

SAVING ENERGY

If you always choose the highest wash cycle, you'll use more hot water and energy. Make sure to buy a dishwasher with other cycles that use less energy and water—as little as 4 gallons—when dishes are less soiled. A delay-start control lets you wash during less-costly off-peak hours. Read the Energy Guide labels for operating costs.

USER-FRIENDLY FEATURES

Angled control panels, large digital displays, wide push buttons, and soft-touch electronic controls are among the design elements you'll want to investigate. Consider elevating your dishwasher 12 to 18 inches to minimize bending as you load and unload. Inside, several models use sensors to measure the soil content of the water and adjust wash cycles to suit. Be sure that detergent and rinse additive dispensers are large enough and conveniently located.

PERFORMANCE APPRAISAL

Look for a dishwasher with multiple wash cycles and types. These features allow you to take special care of a load of your grandmother's crystal, followed by a load of greasy casserole dishes.

Check the sprayer mechanism design. High-performance dishwashers have two or three spray arms that soak

dishes with water from several levels and angles. In the spray arms, smaller holes tend to emit a more forceful spray. A central wash tower may improve washing performance, but you'll lose some rack space.

A twin-pump system drains dirty water faster than a standard single pump. Wash-water filters and internal food disposers are common on many models. Less common is a booster, which heats rinse water to help sanitize dishes without setting your home's water heater higher.

RACKS

Dish and glass racks are basically metal wires coated with nylon or vinyl. The tops of tines wear first; check the cover-age in those areas. Adjustable-height racks add flexibility when you need to load large items or serving pieces. If you like to entertain, you'll appreciate models that hold 12 place settings (most hold 10). Special baskets, hooks, and trays are designed for knives, cooking utensils, and lightweight plastic items that might fly around during washing.

LONGEVITY

Dishwater tubs are made from plastic, porcelain-enameled metal, or stainless steel. Plastic resists chipping and rusting better than enameled metal, but it can discolor. Stainless-steel washtub interiors are durable and easy to rinse and clean, and the finish resists nicks, chips, stains, and odor buildup. Stainless-steel stands up to abuse, so it looks new for a long time, and its natural sheeting action saves drying time.

EXTERIORS

High-end dishwasher models are available in a restaurant-style look. If you want your dishwasher to disappear, choose a built-in model and add trim panels that match your cabinets. Some manufacturers have moved controls from the front to the top of the door to further disguise the dishwasher.

OPPOSITE: **Blend appliances with cabinetry. For a fully integrated style, this dishwasher's controls are on the upper door rim.**

ABOVE LEFT: **A stainless-steel dishwasher provides contemporary contrast in a cottage-style kitchen.**

Keep It Clean. Here's a dishwasher that can handle big and small loads economically. The Fisher & Paykel DishDrawer has two compartments that can operate independently or in tandem. That means you can run a small load if you need to, using as little as 2 gallons of water. Wash pots and pans in one drawer, and delicate crystal in the other using a different cycle. Or load and unload drawers in sequence so you always have clean dishes.

refrigerators
and freezers

Day in and day out, the refrigerator is the kitchen's workhorse, and it's used by every member of the family. Cold storage is packed with cool features, but before you spend $500 to $8,000, it's wise to ponder your priorities.

CONFIGURATIONS

The most popular refrigerator-freezer unit is the two-door, top-freezer design. Bottom-freezer units put fresh food at eye level. Side-by-side models have narrow doors that open at the center. They generally offer more overall storage capacity and easier access for children or people in wheelchairs. However, most of these units have an in-door icemaker on the freezer side, which limits freezer storage space.

SPACE REQUIREMENTS

Refrigerators vary in size and required clearance space. Measure the height, width, and depth of your available refrigerator space and bring these dimensions when you shop. Shallow models that extend about as far as standard cabinet fronts from the wall look better than refrigerators that bump out beyond countertops, blocking traffic or a doorway.

CAPACITY

Refrigerator sizes range from 9 to 30 cubic feet. A family of two generally needs 8 to 10 cubic feet of fresh food space. Add an extra cubic foot for each additional family member. Refrigerators can operate for 15 years or more, so remember to plan for changes in family size.

A family of two needs about 4 cubic feet of freezer space. Add 2 cubic feet for each additional person. Increase the freezer space if you buy a lot of frozen products or shop infrequently. Top- and bottom-mount freezers offer the most storage flexibility. Side-by-side models may offer more storage space, but sometimes it's tricky to wedge in a pizza, party tray, or other large item.

INTERIOR FEATURES

Adjustable-height glass shelves make room for foods of any size and shape and better reveal what you're hungry for. Spillproof shelves reduce cleanup time; look for ones that lift all the way out for washing in the sink. Large, adjustable door bins are essential for easy access to gallon-size milk, juice, and soft drinks. Spacious crispers with clear fronts help you keep track of fruits and vegetables. Adjustable humidity controls keep foods fresh longer. In the freezer, slide- and tilt-out baskets are handy.

ICEMAKERS

Some refrigerator-freezer models have icemakers built into the freezer at the factory. In other models, icemaker kits can be installed quickly.

Once you've used a through-the-door ice and water dispenser, it's hard to imagine life without one. Most useful for children or people who frequently get

Keep It Cold. Do you ever think one refrigerator isn't enough? Wouldn't it be convenient to add a smaller model in an exercise or family room to keep drinks and snacks handy? Several refrigerator manufacturers make refrigerator drawers that fit neatly into cabinetry. You can stack them for a traditional refrigerator configuration, or use them alone. Many people install them in kitchen islands. Drawers are fully built in and hinges are hidden; add hardware to match surrounding cabinets.

cold drinks, these devices save energy—no warm air enters the interior of the unit. High-end refrigerators often include built-in water filters that help the dispensed ice and water look and taste better.

REFRIGERATOR STYLE

You have several options for the look of your refrigerator. Attention-getting stainless steel has made tremendous inroads in the last few years, as have restaurant-style glass doors and wood panels that blend with the surrounding cabinets. White and almond remain the most popular colors, but black is striking and may match your other appliances.

NOISE AND ENERGY ISSUES

When you're in the store, ask that a few models be turned on so you can hear how they sound. The noise will be quieter in your kitchen than on a concrete sales floor. Check each model's yellow Energy Guide label to determine the average energy use per year. Make sure the models you compare are the same capacity.

OPPOSITE: This shallow model refrigerator extends the same distance from the wall as the cabinets on both sides, giving a more streamlined look to the kitchen.

BELOW: Wooden trim panels disguise the refrigerator in this kitchen so that it is virtually indistinguishable from the cabinets.

specialty appliances

Just as more people are multitasking at work and at home—preparing dinner while talking on the phone while catching up on the day's news—more kitchen appliances serve multiple functions. But many specialty appliances on the market also cater to the interests and needs of serious bakers, chefs, and entertainers.

PRO-STYLE SINKS

With other professional-style appliances commonplace in kitchens, pro-style sinks are making a debut in homes. The Pro CookSink and Pro CookCenter by Kohler, for example, offer stainless-steel cooking vessels and touchpad temperature controls to boil water fast. To avoid carrying boiling water from stove to sink, just push a button to drain cooking water.

REFRIGERATOR DRAWERS

These handy appliances are designed to fit into the same space as existing cabinetry and can be stacked as needed. Position the drawers and a microwave oven outside the main work area and

LEFT (TOP AND BOTTOM): **Add refrigerator drawers in a highly used work zone and maximize the efficiency of your kitchen.**

ABOVE: **Install a warming drawer in the island to hold baked goods or side dishes at serving temperature until the main course finishes cooking. Brushed stainless-steel door and drawer pulls are easy to grasp.**

stock with child-friendly foods for a self-serve after-school snack area.

COFFEE BARS

Create an at-home coffee shop with a built-in espresso machine. Commercial-grade espresso machines are available for in-home use by serious coffee lovers. If you don't have that much space to devote to coffee, a plethora of small countertop espresso and coffeemakers are also available. Plan an area of the kitchen to conveniently group all of the items you'll need for your morning coffee ritual. If you prefer a sleek, uncluttered look, keep the items in an appliance garage or an easy-to-access cabinet.

WARMING DRAWERS

For families or anyone who enjoys entertaining, warming drawers are an ideal way to accommodate busy schedules or multiple food preparation times. They maintain the crispness of crisp foods and prevent moist foods from drying out. When entertaining, keep side dishes at serving temperature until the main course is prepared. Drawers are typically available in 30- and 36-inch widths. They're usually finished in stainless steel, but some can accept wood panels for an integrated look with other cabinets.

WINE STORAGE

Wine enthusiasts and those who enjoy entertaining will appreciate the wine refrigerator. These units are outfitted with racks that store wines in the recommended horizontal position so the corks don't dry out or let in air and ruin the wine. The temperature is adjustable. Try a built-in or freestanding unit.

TOP: A beverage cooler and wine rack are welcome additions. Keep glassware in cabinets above, *not shown*.

ABOVE: Tuck a built-in espresso machine near the breakfast table. A warming drawer underneath can hold cups and croissants.

lighting

ABOVE: Although windows and French doors bring abundant natural light into this kitchen, hanging fixtures illuminate countertop work areas.

LEFT: Suspend fixtures so the bottom of the shade is about 28 inches above the work surface. A lower position may obstruct your view across the room, and anything higher can make the fixture seem disconnected from the island. Halogen lamps give a crisp white light that shows off food colors; incandescent lamps, although warm-looking, make colors appear less bold. To set the mood for dining and entertaining, add an easy-to-install dimmer switch.

OPPOSITE: Combination lighting makes it easy to adapt conditions to the changing needs and uses of various work zones throughout the day.

Kitchen lighting needs to be functional and mood-setting. After all, this room serves as a gathering place. A lighting plan that addresses general, ambient, task, and accent lighting will serve you and your cooking and dining space best.

Here are some tips for creating a well-lit, cheerful spot to prepare food, eat meals, and chat with family and friends.

Overhead lighting pours light over the entire room. Well-placed lighting from ceiling-mount fixtures, track lights, or recessed cans provides good overall illumination. Scatter fixtures throughout the room so they pool light where you need it most: over the sink, near the oven, and on the countertops. In kitchens larger than 120 square feet, use two or more ceiling-mount fixtures.

Natural light from windows and skylights makes the most of Mother Nature's sunshine. These panes can bring in bright beams or soft, filtered light. Install curtains or blinds to control the amount of light.

Task lights, such as small pendants or individual recessed cans over the island or sink, throw a spotlight on the work at hand. Choose lights that reflect your personality and the character of the kitchen. Recessed cans with eyeball trims direct light to specific areas.

Undercabinet lights function as task lights for the countertop. Hidden beneath upper cabinets, these recessed fixtures are usually controlled by a switch on the backsplash. Low-voltage halogen "hockey puck" lights can be hidden in the undercabinet recess; track lights also work. An inexpensive option for lighting the countertop uses slimline fluorescent fixtures; install warm-white bulbs for a more natural look.

In-cabinet lights illuminate whatever you have stored in glass-door cabinets. In-cabinet lighting keeps glass-door cabinets from looking like black holes and makes the whole kitchen glow.

Side lighting is the most ignored option. Wall sconces, which diffuse light outward, eliminate the hard shadows that ceiling-mount fixtures can create. One or two well-placed sconces produce face- and food-flattering light.

Ambient lighting, produced by fixtures mounted in the soffit or above upper cabinets, imparts a rich glow to the room. This type of light can emphasize a striking ceiling treatment or supplement the main overhead lighting.

Dimmer switches are a must for kitchen fixtures. At dinner, keep lights bright. At night, when the kitchen is not in use, maintain a soft glow to guide thirsty children in their quest for a glass of water.

New lighting designs are always being introduced, so visit supply stores and showrooms to get a sense of the latest possibilities.

bulb options

Most lamps and fixtures are created for a particular type of lightbulb. Most bulbs are available in various shapes and sizes. Here's what you'll find when you go shopping:

INCANDESCENT. Info: Most commonly used bulb type. **Pros:** Casts a warm, pleasant light. Least expensive. **Cons:** Produces a lot of heat. Can become dim with use.

TUNGSTEN-HALOGEN. Info: Low voltage. Pricier type of incandescent bulb. Produces an intense beam of light. **Pros:** Ideal for accent lighting. Doesn't dim with age. Can last four times as long as incandescent bulbs. Uses less electricity. **Cons:** Light beams can produce an intense amount of heat. Must be used away from fabrics, paper, and flammable materials. Must be handled carefully. Direct contact with skin will contaminate the bulb, damage the glass, and cause it to burn out rapidly.

XENON. Info: Brightness of halogen bulbs without the intense heat and delicate handling requirements. **Pros:** Low voltage. Energy-efficient. **Cons:** Expensive.

FLUORESCENT. Info: Lasts longer in fixtures that aren't turned off and on frequently. For the most pleasing light quality, look for color-corrected or warm white bulbs. **Pros:** Budget-savvy choice. Uses just a third of the electricity and ultimately costs less over time than incandescents. **Cons:** Can cast a harsh light.

windows

Fresh air, views, and natural light are key in any room, but in the kitchen, they take on special importance.

The kitchen is where you come in the morning to wake up. Bountiful sunlight streaming into the space is sure to give your day a cheery start. At the opposite end of the day, unwind while watching the sun go down over dinner. And when somebody burns a roast, ample working windows help eliminate the smoke and smell.

An ideal time to enlarge, add, or reconfigure windows is during an overall kitchen remodeling. Place a bay window with a garden view in a bump-out designed for eating. Install skylights overhead. Enlarge the over-the-sink window so you can enjoy even more of the outdoors.

WINDOW SHOPPING

Like many products, windows aren't what they used to be—and that's a good thing. Refined materials and improved details put a lot more control at your fingertips. You get a wider variety of standard shapes, sizes, and designs, and all of them are engineered for performance levels that older windows just can't match.

For starters, here's a look at the five most common window categories:

Double-hung and single-hung: This traditional design is still the most common. Double-hung windows have a pair of movable sashes that slide vertically within the frame; single-hung models also feature an upper and lower sash, but only the lower sash is operative. (Because production volume typically is higher for double-hungs, single-hung windows usually offer little or no cost advantage.)

Appropriate for all but the most contemporary homes, double-hung and single-hung windows can be found on Cape Cods, Colonials, Victorians, early-20th-century bungalows, and other "period" architectural styles. Muntin, or grille, designs provide stylistic cues, but the basic design remains versatile.

LEFT: Situating the work areas toward the center of the kitchen left room for this window-side breakfast nook.

ABOVE: A bank of windows overlooking a garden or yard makes a sunny, ideal spot for a kitchen sink.

open as fully as casements, but they offer the advantage of shedding water harmlessly if left open during a rainfall.

Though they can be used alone, awning windows often are installed above or below large picture windows to provide ventilation at the top or bottom of a wall.

Like casements, awning windows take on a more traditional flavor when fitted with muntins but look contemporary when left unadorned.

Gliding: The principle of a gliding window, where one or two sashes slide horizontally in the tracks of a frame, has a long history that includes Japanese shoji. As with awning windows, gliders have a horizontal orientation, so they often work best with home designs that have strong horizontal lines, such as ranches or Prairie-style buildings.

Picture: They don't get any simpler than this. Picture windows are stationary (inoperative) windows used for light and views only. They don't have to be large but often are. When maximum views are the objective, a picture window offers the least obstruction. Ventilation requirements are often handled by installing operative windows above, below, or alongside a picture window.

As with other window types, picture windows impart a decidedly modern feel when they're large and uninterrupted by muntins. Smaller picture windows with grilles and appropriate trim can imitate most traditional looks.

Specialty: Just about anything outside these five categories qualifies as a specialty window. This term refers to unusual shapes, such as round, half-round, and other nonstandard configurations. Most are fixed-sash and are included to create architectural interest.

Other specialty windows include bow and bay windows, preassembled

Casement: Casement windows pivot on hinges, somewhat as doors do, but they usually swing outward and are controlled by a hand-crank mechanism affixed to the windowsill. Casement shapes tend toward the tall and narrow, so wide wall openings usually feature multiples, sometimes with a fixed picture window in the center. Ventilation is generous relative to the overall window area because the entire sash swings open, but

exposure of the outward-swinging frame can be a problem if rain arrives suddenly.

Ranch-style, Prairie-style, and other 20th-century homes often feature this type of window. Grilles help create a traditional look, while an unbroken expanse of glass provides a contemporary flavor.

Awning: This is another type of hinged window, but one that pivots at the top. With their horizontal rather than vertical orientation, awnings don't

groupings that change the profile of an exterior wall.

Though substantially more costly than standard windows, these variations provide more light and ventilation in a given amount of wall area and create a more spacious feel and room for window seats.

WINDOW MATERIALS

Virtually any good-quality window should be fitted with insulated glass. This means the glazing is a sandwich of two panes of glass separated by "warm channel" spacers. The spacers act as thermal breaks to keep the exchange of inside and outside temperatures to a minimum. The voids between the panes are sometimes filled with argon gas, which offers better insulating properties than ordinary air. Unless you're ordering custom windows, standard units will likely be dual-glazed and argon-filled, and perhaps will have a low-E coating (for low emissivity, which inhibits the transfer of radiant solar heat).

The frame components that secure the glazing give the window its structure and operation. Wood has been the tradi-

Designer Tip

If you're remodeling a kitchen, stick with the predominant window type used in the rest of the house. Mixing window styles creates a patchwork look on a home's exterior. If you are adding a breakfast room, for instance, repeat muntin styles or other details for consistency.

tional material for the jambs, sash frames, sills, and trim, but its maintenance requirements and the inevitable problems with water and sun damage have brought changes. Protecting wood with a weatherproof covering called cladding eliminates the need for painting and protects the window from the elements.

There are two types of cladding: vinyl and aluminum. Vinyl offers the advantages of excellent impact resistance and integral color, so scratches on the surface won't expose the layer underneath. Color choices from most manufacturers are limited to white, a dark taupe, and a lighter neutral color.

Aluminum cladding requires more care in handling to avoid scratches or dents, but the factory-applied paint

finishes are extremely durable and typically come in at least a dozen colors.

The interior surfaces of these windows are finish-grade wood that can be stained or painted.

Some manufacturers do without wood entirely, opting for frame components made of aluminum or solid vinyl. Though less expensive, these have their drawbacks, too. Aluminum is a poor insulator, and vinyl lacks the rigidity of either wood or aluminum, so the frames flex more and move in response to temperature swings.

Wood composites have become more common for the structural core of window frames and components. These compounds are extruded into hollow tube shapes, then covered with vinyl or aluminum cladding on the exterior and a paint primer or vinyl cladding on the interior. This approach capitalizes on

BELOW: **It's difficult to imagine that this sunny, organized kitchen was once two small rooms with only one tiny window in the cooking space. Removing walls and wrapping one side of the room with glass opened up the kitchen.**

the strength and insulating properties of wood but doesn't require the expensive, high-grade materials used in solid-wood frames; however, you can't use a transparent stain on interior surfaces.

Depending on what style, features, and materials you choose, costs for windows vary widely. You generally get what you pay for. Energy efficiency and a no-maintenance exterior will offset the up-front cost over time. Installation and labor costs could be higher for an economy-grade window if you factor in charges for painting. And if economy-grade windows are leaking and rotten in just a few years and have to be replaced, they were no bargain.

cost guide

CABINETS: (per linear foot) $60–$200 **for fixed-size stock** (ready-made), limited finish and door-style selection. $100–$650 **for semicustom** (fixed sizes with fill-in panels to fit space available), broad choice of finishes and styles. $500–$1,200 **for custom** (any size, shape, style, finish you want).

COUNTERTOPS: (per linear foot) $10–$50 **for laminate, ceramic tile.** $100–$150 **for solid-surfacing.** $50+ **for butcher block.** $70–$200 **for marble, granite.** (Per square foot) $65+ **for stainless steel.** $60–$130 **for concrete.**

COOKTOP: $250–$450 **for basic** four-burner model, electric or gas. $450–$1,200 **for glass, ceramic, radiant, halogen.** $2,500–$4,800 **for high-powered** professional-grade.

DISHWASHER: $300–$500 **for basic model,** plastic or enameled-steel interior. $600–$850 **for midrange** with built-in disposer, pot-scrubber cycle, programmable feature. $1,000–$2,500 **for stainless-steel interior,** ultraquiet feature.

FAUCET: $60–$150 **for basic chrome** with plastic cartridge. $150–$350 **for solid brass,** ceramic-disk valves, chrome/color finish, pull-out spout. $200–$350 **for brass, nickel, copper, pewter, brushed, matte** finishes, pullout spout. $500–$1,000 **for contemporary** wall-mount design.

FLOORING: (per square foot) $1–$5 **for vinyl tile or vinyl sheet flooring.** $3–$12 **for ceramic tile, slate.** $4–$11 **for laminate.** $4–$9 **for cork.** $6–$14 **for hardwood.** $5–$30+ **for marble and granite.** $4–$11 **for linoleum.**

GARBAGE DISPOSAL: $75–$100 **for a basic,** batch-feed model. $300–$500 **for a top-of-the-line,** high-power, quiet-running, continuous-feed model.

MICROWAVE OVEN: $70–$100 **for basic** countertop model. $200–$450 **for high-powered, programmable** with turntable. $600–$1,500 **for built-in.**

OVEN: $400–$1,000 **for basic,** single model slide-in or built-in. $1,000–$1,500 **for double, self-cleaning.** $2,000+ **for single, microwave-convection combination.**

RANGE: (cooktop and oven are one unit) $300–$550 **for basic 30-inch model,** electric or gas. $400–$2,500 **for self-cleaning,** smooth-top glass or sealed burners. $1,000–$9,000 **for dual-fuel.** $4,000–$9,000+ **for pro-style.**

REFRIGERATOR-FREEZER: $550–$750 **for basic model,** freezer on top. $600–$1,200 **for side-by-side.** $1,200–$3,000 **for 22-cubic-foot model,** top-mount with convenience features. $3,000–$8,000 **for built-in** or commercial-style.

SINK: $100–$200 **for enameled steel.** $150–$400 **for acrylic.** $200–$1,200 **for cast iron or solid-surfacing.** $65–$2,000 **for stainless steel.** $750–$2,000+ **for apron-front** ("farmhouse") style.

TRASH COMPACTOR: $500–$1,400

VENTILATION HOOD: $75–$400 **for basic** hood fan, light. $500–$1,000 **for premium** updraft, downdraft. $500–$1,000 **for slide-out.** $1,000–$5,000 **for high-capacity,** suitable for professional-caliber range.

everything in its place

Once you've explored layout options, turn to established design guidelines to develop an effective kitchen. »

The National Kitchen and Bath Association (NKBA) creates basic design standards that help define the most efficient and effective kitchen layouts. For more information about kitchen design, products, and other issues, and more specific design guidelines, contact the NKBA at 687 Willow Grove St., Hackettstown, NJ 07840. Call: 800/843-6522 or visit www.nkba.org.

kitchen
design guidelines

GUIDELINES FOR TRAFFIC AND WORK FLOW

Doorways should be at least 32 inches wide and not more than 24 inches deep. When two counters flank a doorway entry, the minimum 32-inch-wide clearance should be allowed from a point of one counter closest to the doorway to the closest point of the counter on the opposite side.

Walkways (passages between vertical objects greater than 24 inches deep where not more than one is a work counter or appliance) should be 36 inches wide.

Work aisles (passages between vertical objects, both of which are work counters or appliances) should be at least 42 inches wide in one-cook kitchens and at least 48 inches wide in multiple-cook kitchens.

The work triangle (the line drawn between the center of the sink to the center of the fridge to the center of the primary cooking surface, then back to the sink's center) should be no more than 26 feet, with no single leg of the work triangle shorter than 4 feet or longer than 9 feet. The work triangle should not intersect an island or peninsula by more than 12 inches.

If two or more people cook at the same time, a work triangle should be placed for each cook. One leg of the primary and secondary triangles may be shared, but the two should not cross one another. Appliances may be shared

OPPOSITE: Solve storage problems with island shelves and drawers. A curvaceous glass-top counter accommodates seating.

or separate.

No major traffic patterns should cross through the work triangle.

No entry, appliance, or cabinet doors should interfere with another.

In a seating area, 32 inches of clearance should be allowed from the counter or table edge to any wall or obstruction behind it if no traffic will pass behind a seated diner. If there is a walkway behind the seating area, 65 inches of clearance, total, including the walkway, should be allowed between the seating area and any wall or obstruction.

GUIDELINES FOR STORAGE

Kitchen storage guidelines from the NKBA include a basic calculation to determine wall and base cabinets, shelves, drawers, pantry, and miscellaneous storage. Storage is described in terms of the number of inches of shelf and drawer frontage.

The calculation to determine shelf-and-drawer-frontage inches is:

Cabinet width in inches×number of shelves/drawers×cabinet depth in feet=shelf/drawer frontage.

Example: A 36-inch-wide, 2-foot-deep base cabinet with 3 shelves is calculated as follows:

36×3×2=216 frontage inches

Small kitchens (less than 150 square feet): Allow approximately 1,400 shelf and drawer frontage inches. The inches should be divided among wall, base, drawer, pantry, and miscellaneous storage, with the highest percentage (approximately 35 to 40 percent) for base cabinets. Wall cabinets should account for approximately 20 percent and drawers approximately 25 percent of storage. Pantry space can account for approximately 10 to 15 percent, with the remainder for miscellaneous storage. Any storage space more than 84 inches above the floor is miscellaneous.

Medium kitchens (151 to 350 square feet): Allow approximately 1,700 inches of shelf and drawer frontage. Use the same percentages as for the small kitchen, above, to allocate the storage space among wall, base, drawer, pantry, and miscellaneous categories.

Large kitchens (more than 350 square feet): Allow approximately 2,000 inches of shelf and drawer frontage. Allocate the space accordingly: Base cabinets should account for approximately one-third of the frontage. Drawers can account for approximately 25 percent of storage and wall cabinets for approximately 20 percent. Pantry space will take about 15 percent of the total, with the remainder for miscellaneous storage.

At least five storage or organizing items located between 15 and 48 inches

above the finished floor (or extending into that area) should be included in the kitchen to improve functionality and accessibility. These items may include, but are not limited to, lowered wall cabinets, raised base cabinets, tall cabinets, appliance garages, bins and racks, swing-out pantries, interior vertical dividers, and specialized drawers and shelves. Full-extension drawers and

roll-out shelves greater than the 120-inch minimum for small kitchens or 165 inches for larger kitchens may also be included.

For kitchens with usable corner areas in the plan, at least one functional corner storage unit should be included.

The top edge of a waste receptacle should be no higher than 36 inches. The receptacle should be easily accessible

and should be removable without raising the receptacle bottom higher than the unit's physical height. Lateral removal of the receptacle, which doesn't require lifting, is preferred.

GUIDELINES FOR COUNTER SURFACE AND LANDING SPACE
At least two work-counter heights should be installed in the kitchen for

different uses and functions, with one 28 to 36 inches above the finished floor and the other 36 to 45 inches above the finished floor.

Countertop frontage: Small, medium, and large kitchens should all allow at least 158 inches of countertop frontage. Counters must be a minimum of 24 inches deep, and wall cabinets must be at least 15 inches above the counter surface for the counter to be included in the total frontage measurement. Measure only countertop frontage; do not count corner space.

If an appliance garage or storage cabinet extends to the counter, the countertop frontage can still be counted, but work space will be minimized in that location.

Space near primary sinks: There should be at least 24 inches of countertop frontage on one side of the primary sink and 18 inches on the other side (including corner sink applications), with the 24-inch counter frontage at the same counter height as the sink. Countertop frontage may be a continuous surface or the total of two angled countertop sections. Measure only countertop frontage; do not count corner space.

The minimum allowable space from a corner to the edge of the primary sink is 3 inches; it should also be a minimum of 15 inches from that corner to the sink's centerline.

If there is anything less than 18 inches of frontage from the edge of the primary sink to a corner, 21 inches of clear counter (measure frontage) should be allowed on the return.

Space near secondary sinks: At least 3 inches of countertop frontage should be provided on one side of secondary sinks and 18 inches on the other side (including corner sink applications), with the 18 inch counter frontage at the same counter height as the sink. The countertop frontage may be a continuous surface or the total of two angled countertop sections. Measure only countertop frontage; do not count corner space.

Space near cooking surfaces: In an open-ended kitchen configuration, at least 12 inches of counter space should be allowed on one side of the cooking

OPPOSITE: **Pull stools up to a generous work island and signal its multipurpose nature. The glamorous granite top invites socializing and provides a tough surface for food preparation. Roomy cabinets hide bulky kitchen equipment.**

LEFT: **The right touches make all the difference. Rich cherry cabinets and artistic light fixtures create an elegant atmosphere in an otherwise utilitarian U-shape kitchen.**

surface and at least 15 inches on the other.

For an enclosed configuration, follow the appliance manufacturer's instructions or local codes for the distance between the appliance and the end wall protected by flame-retardant surfacing material. These guidelines may not allow for enough landing space on the end wall side of the appliance. On the other side of the appliance allow 15 inches at the same counter height as the appliance. For safety reasons, the countertop should also extend a minimum of 9 inches behind the cooking surface, at the same counter height as the appliance, in any instance where there is not an abutting wall or backsplash.

In an outside-angle installation of cooking surfaces, there should be at least 12 inches of straight counter space on one side and 15 inches of straight counter space on the other side, at the same counter height as the appliance.

Space near refrigerators: Allow for at least 15 inches of counter space on the latch side of the refrigerator or on either side of a side-by-side refrigerator, or at least 15 inches of landing space that is no more than 48 inches across from the refrigerator.

Space near ovens: Although it is not ideal, it is acceptable to place an oven adjacent to a refrigerator. For convenience, the refrigerator should be the appliance placed next to the available countertop. If there is no safe landing area across from the oven, this arrangement may be reversed.

Allow for at least 15 inches of landing space that is at least 16 inches deep next to or above the oven if the appliance door opens into a primary traffic pattern. At least 15×16 inches of landing space that is no more than 48 inches across from the oven is acceptable if the appliance does not open into

a traffic area.

Plan for at least 36 inches of continuous countertop that is at least 16 inches deep for the preparation center. The preparation center should be immediately adjacent to a water source.

At least 15 inches of landing space, a minimum of 16 inches deep, should be planned above, below, or adjacent to a microwave oven.

Space near food preparation area: The preparation center can be placed between the primary sink and the cooking surface, between the refrigerator and the primary sink, or adjacent to a secondary sink on an island or other cabinet section.

General countertop guidelines: No two primary work centers (the main sink, refrigerator, preparation, or cooktop/range center) should be separated by a full-height, full-depth tall tower, such as an oven cabinet, pantry cabinet, or refrigerator.

Countertop corners should be clipped or curved; counter edges should be eased to eliminate sharp corners.

GUIDELINES FOR APPLIANCE PLACEMENT AND APPLIANCE CLEARANCE SPACE

Knee space, which may be open or adaptable, should be planned below or adjacent to sinks, cooktops, ranges, and ovens whenever possible. Knee space should be a minimum of 27 inches high by 30 inches wide by 19 inches deep under the counter. The 27-inch height may decrease progressively as depth increases. Surfaces in the knee space area should be finished for safety and aesthetic purposes.

Allow for a clear floor space of 30×48 inches at the sink, dishwasher, cooktop, oven, and refrigerator. These spaces may overlap, and up to 19 inches of knee space beneath an appliance, counter cabinet, and so on, may be part

of the total 30-inch and/or 48-inch dimension.

Dishwashers: Allow for a minimum of 21 inches of clear floor space between the edge of the dishwasher and counters, appliances, and/or cabinets that are placed at a right angle to the dishwasher.

The edge of the primary dishwasher should be within 36 inches of the edge of one sink. The dishwasher should be accessible to more than one person at a time to accommodate other cooks, kitchen cleanup helpers, and/or other family members.

Sinks: If the kitchen has only one sink, it should be located between or across from the cooking surface, preparation area, or refrigerator.

Cooking surfaces: Allow at least 24 inches of clearance between the cooking surface and a protected surface above, or at least 30 inches of clearance between the cooking surface and an unprotected surface above. If the protected surface is a microwave hood combination, manufacturer's specifications may dictate a smaller clearance.

Ventilation systems: All major appliances used for surface cooking should have a ventilation system that follows the recommendations of the appliance manufacturer. General guidelines suggest a fan rated at 150 cubic feet of air per minute minimum.

Windows: Do not place the cooking surface below an operable window. Windows, operative or inoperative, above a cooking surface should not be dressed with flammable window treatments.

Microwave ovens: Place the microwave oven 3 inches below the shoulder of the primary user, but not more than 54 inches above the floor and not less than 15 inches above the floor.

OPPOSITE: **Peninsulas help separate and define the work zones in this kitchen in a contemporary home.**

plumbing and electric

As fun as it is to contemplate having beautiful cabinetry and countertops and gleaming faucets and flooring, the least glamorous of kitchen-remodeling decisions are critical to make before any remodeling begins. Evaluate your home's plumbing and electrical systems and plan for adding or changing them to accommodate the new elements.

PLUMBING

If you're gutting the space and starting over, save money by leaving plumbing lines where they are, but if you're moving the sink or adding one, both water pipes and drains will have to be moved.

Perhaps the biggest plumbing issue in kitchen remodeling (especially if you're rearranging the elements of your kitchen) is how far the sink trap can stray from the vertical stack—also called a soil stack. The sink trap is a curved section of drain pipe that holds enough standing water to make an airtight seal, which prevents sewer gases from backing up and leaking into your home. The stack is the typically 40-inch fixed pipe that all of the usually 1½-inch sink pipes in the home flow into; it takes liquid and solid waste out of the house and into the sewer or septic system.

Local plumbing codes require that a

sink trap be located within a specified distance of the stack. Your plumber will have to install your sink so that it is in compliance with local code.

ELECTRICAL

If you're enlarging the size of your kitchen or adding features, you'll need to increase the amount of amperage allotted to the space. If you own an older home, you may already be aware of this—if, for instance, you have inconveniently blown a fuse when the toaster and microwave oven were being used at the same time.

With a kitchen plan in hand, sit down with your contractor and/or electrician and go over locations for each electrical outlet and telephone and television jack you plan to have.

Some appliances and electrical systems require special considerations, and many of the heaviest hitters in the wattage-requirement department are used in the kitchen: the refrigerator,

Outlet Options: The number of electrical outlets you need will depend somewhat on the size of your kitchen, of course, but generally, a well-outfitted kitchen requires up to seven individual circuits: a 120/240-volt circuit for an electric range, two separate 120-volt circuits for the dishwasher and microwave, one circuit for the refrigerator, at least two 120-volt small-appliance circuits above the countertop, and one general lighting circuit to supply all the lights with electricity.

Countertop outlets can be no more than 4 feet apart so that, measuring horizontally, no point on the counter is more than 24 inches from an outlet.

Designer Tip

Designating the operation of all of your kitchen lighting onto a single keypad is a great benefit. Prewiring for this system requires a specific plan; you'll need to discuss this with your electrician.

microwave oven, and toaster, for instance. A floor-warming system—often installed under ceramic tile to take the chill off its surface—may require its own circuit, and a stove or an electric dryer requires its own 240-volt circuit. In addition, be sure ground fault circuit interrupters (GFCI) are specified for all electrical outlets.

If you're planning an Internet-accessible computer in the kitchen, allow hookups for that, whether you use a phone line, DSL, or cable modem.

You'll need to determine the sites of electrical outlets before wall tiles or backsplashes are installed. Remember that electrical equipment such as toasters and mixers should be used far from open flames or the heat of the stove; they also should be used nowhere near running water. Be sure to discuss these issues with the electrician who will be wiring your kitchen.

Ideally, electrical sockets should be situated near the cabinets where small appliances are stored and over the countertops or other work surfaces where they are usually used so that you don't have to lift and haul hand mixers, bread machines, and food processors across the kitchen. Electrical outlets should also be placed at a height that allows the appliances to be used easily without the cord snaking around and cluttering the countertop.

If possible, have your electrician place the sockets at such a height that the cord lengths on your small appliances, such as toaster and coffeemakers, can be shortened, making them tidy and efficient to use.

OPPOSITE: **Having a second sink in a prep station allows a kitchen to easily accommodate a second cook. It also increases remodeling plumbing expenses to run additional water pipes and drains.**

LEFT: **Consider and plan for electrical needs. This custom cabinet was designed as a built-in baking center complete with ample electrical outlets for the appliances used there.**

universal

In most homes, the kitchen harbors irritating barriers for anyone who is in a wheelchair or has other physical limitations. Cabinets and appliances are out of reach. Oven doors drop open and block access to the racks. Countertops are too high. And appliance knobs and faucets can be difficult to operate.

In the past decade, considerable research has been conducted to find ways to make life in the kitchen easier for people with disabilities. Because it is such a complex room, manufacturers of cabinetry, appliances, and plumbing fixtures have teamed with organizations such as the Center for Universal Design and the Paralyzed Veterans of America to find ways to make tasks more comfortable, more convenient, and safer. Here are some ways they've discovered to make your kitchen more user-friendly.

CABINETRY AND COUNTERTOPS

Take advantage of the specialty fittings that cabinetry manufacturers offer. Lazy Susans and pullout shelves bring cabinet contents into view and within reach. Pullout cutting boards can be removed and set on the lap of a seated cook.

If possible, install cabinet doors that slide horizontally, rather than pivoting outward. Choose wide pulls rather than knobs to help people with hand-strength or dexterity problems.

Install a continuous line of countertop—absent of any obstructions—from the refrigerator to the sink to the cooktop to allow the cook to slide mixing and cooking vessels from one workstation to another.

Plan for at least 1½ feet of countertop adjacent to the refrigerator. This surface should be on the opening side of the fridge. If possible, the cooktop and

oven should have about 2 feet of clear countertop surface on each side so that hot dishes can be set down. A right-handed cook needs 3 feet of work surface to the right of the sink and 2 feet of workspace to the left. A left-handed cook requires the opposite configuration.

Leave plenty of knee space under countertops to accommodate wheelchair

Designer Tip

For more information about designing a barrier-free kitchen, contact the National Kitchen and Bath Association at 687 Willow Grove St., Hackettstown, NJ 07840; phone: 800/843-6522; Internet address: www.nkba.org. Or contact The Center for Universal Design, North Carolina State University, 50 Pullen Road, Brooks Hall Room 104, Campus Box 8613, Raleigh, NC 27695-8613; phone: 800/647-6777; Internet address: www.design.ncsu.edu/cud.

users. The minimum measurements for knee space are 30 inches wide, 19 inches deep, and 27 inches high.

Keep most countertops at the standard height. To accommodate a person in a wheelchair, consider lowering one section of countertop, perhaps a peninsula or island. Alternatively, equip the kitchen with a cart that's a convenient height for a seated cook. Adjustable countertops are available on the market, but they are costly. The electronic systems can raise and lower counters to fit the height of each cook in the family.

APPLIANCES AND SINKS

Choose a side-by-side refrigerator model to give a seated cook easy access. Models with ice and water dispensers in

design

the door are especially convenient.

Plan for a separate cooktop and built-in wall oven. The cooktop can be installed at any height, and knee space can be provided beneath it. Smooth glass-top models let the cook easily slide pots and pans. Choose a model with controls at the front so the cook doesn't have to reach across burners. Built-in ovens also can be installed at the most convenient height. Be sure there is a landing space for hot pans and casseroles directly beside or in front of the oven.

Select a basin that is shallow and has the drain at the back to allow adequate knee space below. The area beneath the basin should be insulated to protect legs and feet from contact with hot and cold water pipes.

Provide easy control of water temperature and flow with lever-handle faucets. A gooseneck faucet or one with a retractable or pullout sprayhead makes it easier to fill tall pots.

OPPOSITE: Make a home in the island for the oven, a compact freezer, and small appliances that would otherwise have to occupy countertop space.

ABOVE RIGHT: Position the microwave oven in a midlevel cabinet low enough for the cook to reach but still providing clearance for the door to open without hitting knees.

RIGHT: Wide aisles easily accomodate a wheelchair and lend luxurious spaciousness to this kitchen. The microwave resides in a midlevel cabinet low enough for the main chef in the family to access from his wheelchair, but high enough to provide knee clearance when the door is open.

design your layout

Create an ideal kitchen that meets functional cooking and storage needs with personal style. »

>> A successful kitchen remodeling starts with a clear picture of the space available—the dimensions of your blank canvas. Forget about existing cabinets, counters, appliances, and other components. Simply imagine an empty room—nothing but walls, windows, floor, and ceiling. Then turn your imagination into a plan of action with a floor plan of your existing kitchen.

measuring
your space

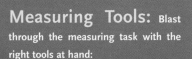

RIGHT: **It's a good idea to measure a couple of times to make sure your measurements are accurate, particularly if your measurements reveal flaws such as walls not plumb or floors not level.**

Measuring Tools: Blast through the measuring task with the right tools at hand:

- 25-foot steel tape measure
- Sharp pencil
- 1/4-inch graph paper
- A few sheets of tracing paper
- A good-quality artist's eraser
- 12-inch architect's combination ruler and scale
- Triangle

To get the best picture of what you have to work with, carefully measure your kitchen space and draw an accurate, scaled floor plan. (See pages 126–127 for further information about floor plans, and samples of floor plans and elevations.) If you have the original blueprints of your house, you have a jump start on the measuring project, but you still have to check the plans against the actual dimensions to make sure the room was built as shown. Measuring also can reveal flaws—walls not plumb, corners not square, floors not level—that can affect both the final cabinet dimensions and how the cabinets are installed.

GETTING STARTED

Choose a steel measuring tape, preferably at least 25 feet long, instead of a yardstick or cloth tape. Record measurements in inches and feet. You'll use both in the planning process. Cabinets and appliances, for example, are measured in inches.

HOW TO MEASURE YOUR SPACE

Carefully measure the perimeter dimensions of the room. Draw an outline of the space on ¼-inch graph paper, using a scale of ¼ inch per foot. A ruler and triangle will help you keep lines straight and corners perpendicular.

Measure and draw the room's more detailed dimensions. Start in a corner and work your way around the room in one direction. Place the tape against the wall, 36 inches from the floor, and measure from corner to trim edge of the nearest doorway or window. Note the measurement to the nearest ¹⁄₁₆ inch. Be sure to measure the width of the trim.

Measure and note the location and width of each doorway and window (the space between the inside edges of the

trim). Also note the hinging and swing of each door and to which side the door extends.

Measure from the floor to the bottom edge of the trim under the windowsill. For any window that is over a counter, the distance between the sill and the countertop will be the height of the backsplash.

Measure the height of the room from floor to ceiling. Take this measurement in all corners and at midpoints in each wall, checking to see if the floor is level. Note any discrepancies.

With the help of a partner, measure from a couple of points along a wall to the same points on the opposite wall (again, 36 inches from the floor). Doing so will reveal if either wall is bowed. If

possible, take diagonal, corner-to-corner measurements to see if the room is evenly square. If the two diagonal measurements are not the same in a rectangular or square room, find out the degree of error in each corner by using the 3-4-5 right triangle method: Measure 3 feet out from the corner on one wall and 4 feet out on the other. If the corner is square, the distance between these two points will be exactly 5 feet. If it's more or less, determine the extent of the error on the "short" wall, that is, the one where a cabinet run terminates or has the shorter of the two runs to that corner. Adjusting the cabinets on the shorter length will require less effort.

Measure and note the exact locations and dimensions of radiators,

registers, switches, receptacles, light fixtures, and, if possible, places where plumbing and gas connections come through the wall or floor.

When you finish a wall, add up the individual measurements and check the total against your original measurement of the entire wall. If there's any difference, start over.

Once you complete your sketch of the room, draw detailed elevation views, (including doorways, windows, and permanent fixtures).

ABOVE: **If you have your heart set on an island, make sure it will fit with plenty of work flow and traffic flow space around it.**

planning
cabinets

Designer Tip

Many homeowners find deep drawer bases in a 24- to 36-inch width are useful for storing dishes, pots, and pans. Thirty-six-inch bases with five shallow drawers are well-suited to storing linens.

DREAMING AND DRAWING

Now you're ready to work with the layout. After you've drawn an accurate floor plan, you and/or your design pro can use it as a guide for sketching ideas. Lay tracing paper over the drawing and pencil in various layouts.

Maybe that U-shape kitchen has room for an island. Perhaps a peninsula could turn your L-shape kitchen into a full or partial U.

As you develop favorite arrangements, you'll want to become familiar with standard appliance and cabinetry dimensions. Check your plans against recommended guidelines listed in Kitchen Design Guidelines, pages 86–91. And if you want to change the location of a sink or a fixed electrical or gas appliance, call your local government to ensure that you'll be complying with building code. It's much easier and cheaper to change plans now rather than later.

LAYING OUT CABINETS

Your choices in kitchen cabinetry may seem endless, but cabinet sizes are fairly standardized. Most fixtures and appliances have been sized to coordinate with standard cabinet dimensions. All stock and ready-to-assemble (RTA) and the majority of semicustom and custom

cabinetry lines conform to these standards. You can buy or build cabinetry to nonstandard dimensions if needed, of course.

If ready-made cabinets are your choice, you'll find that base and wall cabinets come in widths that vary in 3-inch increments, typically from 9 to 48 inches. Filler strips that match the cabinet finish fill gaps that inevitably

occur between corner walls and the end of a cabinet run.

BASE CABINETS

Base cabinets are 24 inches deep and 34½ inches high. (With a 1½-inch counter on top, the cabinet height reaches the standard 36 inches.) Keep in mind that base cabinets less than 15 inches wide are useful for little other

than vertical tray storage, so choose the number of narrow units carefully.

WALL CABINETS

Most wall cabinets are 12 to 13 inches deep and 30 to 42 inches high. Thirty-six inches is a popular height in a kitchen with an 8-foot ceiling, leaving room for either a soffit or an open space between the cabinet and ceiling. However, installing a 42-inch wall cabinet running right up to the top of an 8-foot ceiling makes room for an additional shelf inside.

REFRIGERATOR CABINETS

Refrigerator cabinets are a dimensional cross between wall and base cabinets. The actual cabinet portion is mounted over the refrigerator and is as deep as the appliance. These cabinets generally measure 36 inches wide and 18 inches high. If you'll be ordering a refrigerator cabinet, installing the cabinet with a rollout storage fitting will make the deep space far more accessible.

PANTRY CABINETS

Thanks to the many pullout storage fittings available, a high-capacity pantry can be had in just a sliver of space. Pantry cabinet widths range in 3-inch increments from 15 to 36 inches. Most, up to 30 inches wide, stand 84 inches high. Thirty-six-inch pantries generally stand 90 inches high, and 42-inch pantries, 96 inches high. Most pantry cabinets are available with shelves or foldout chef's pantry fittings—or can be left open to serve as broom/utility closets.

OPPOSITE TOP: **A narrow cabinet fitted with several full-extension drawers allows you to organize lots of little things and get to them easily.**

OPPOSITE BOTTOM: **Try to plan a run of cabinets to optimize wall space and maximize storage space but minimize the need for custom cabinetry sizes.**

Fine-Tuning Cabinet Faces. At this point, the biggest variable is cabinet configuration. Here are some tips for fine-tuning your cabinet faces.

- Base cabinets up to 21 inches wide carry one door or a single bank of drawers.
- Doors shouldn't be any wider than 21 inches or they'll swing too far out into the kitchen. Drawer cabinets can be much wider, up to 36 inches.
- Stock and ready-to-assemble wall cabinets can be up to 21 inches wide in a single door style, but it's a good idea to keep them at 18 inches or less. The main drawback to a wider door is that when it swings out, it is awkward looking and can hurt someone who stands up beneath the open door.
- Avoid colliding drawers by keeping drawer cabinets away from inside corners.
- For an orderly appearance, keep doors and drawers in vertical and horizontal alignment.

ABOVE: **Particularly in a large kitchen, cabinets don't need to cover every wall surface. Assess your need for storage prior to planning cabinetry. Here, strategically placed wall cabinets allow plenty of room for a bank of windows along one wall.**

work centers:
food storage and prep

Just as the kitchen's work triangle has three points—the cooktop or range, sink, and refrigerator—the kitchen itself has three work centers: food storage and preparation, cooking, and cleanup. Here are some points to keep in mind when designing the food-prep center.

Although many busy families eat reheated takeout food or pre-prepared meals from the grocery store more often than dinners made from scratch, it's still important to have ample food storage and preparation space. This work center should be equipped for weekend cooks who enjoy making big meals.

Be sure to plan well-organized storage for canned and dry goods, mixing bowls, casserole dishes, cookbooks, and small appliances. A pantry with roll-out shelving makes reaching that can of soup in the back of the cupboard a snap.

Situate the primary food storage near the longest stretch of countertop for easy access to items while cooking. The best places for food storage are cabinets attached to cool outside walls near shaded north-facing windows. Cabinets and walls near heat sources—such as the dishwasher, oven, or refrigerator—are not ideal places for storing foods.

Consider a snack center, which might have a small microwave oven, a wrapping station for lunches and leftovers, a small refrigerator or cooling drawer, and even a second sink. Putting one section of countertop lower than the rest creates a place for kids to make their own snacks.

The latch side of the refrigerator should face into the work triangle. The door should open completely so the bins can be pulled out easily. The refrigerator door should not swing into a doorway.

BELOW: A compact space must work efficiently. Here, the refrigerator, countertop, and sink form a small but hardworking drink-making station.

OPPOSITE: Store food and beverages where they're likely to be used. An under-counter refrigerator drawer holds milk below the espresso maker and cereal canisters.

work centers:
cooking

The main ingredients of the cooking center are the cooktop or range and the microwave oven. Be sure your cooking center has ample storage for all the tools of the cooking trade: pots and pans, utensils, pot holders, hot pads, spices and seasonings, and food products that go directly from the storage container into the simmering pot.

A cooktop is safest and most efficient with at least 18 inches of counterspace on each side. This enables you to turn handles away from traffic and provides a landing space for hot pots. Use a heat-resistant countertop surface around the cooktop or range.

Whether you have a cooktop or a range, the cooking center always requires a ventilation system. The number of Btus put off by your cooktop will determine the strength of ventilation required. A standard four-burner residential range needs a system that blows a minimum of 150 cubic feet of air per minute. Professional-style cooktops and ranges require more ventilation. See pages 69-70 for more information about ventilation systems.

BELOW: A stainless-steel, professional-grade gas range is the focal point of this kitchen. Ample counter space on each side of the range is convenient for transferring hot pots. Frequently used cooking utensils are also stowed adjacent to the range.

OPPOSITE: A ceiling-hung rack is a convenient spot to store pots and pans within easy reach of the cooking center.

work centers:
cleanup

The sink is the centerpiece of the cleanup center. It also is an integral element of the food preparation and cooking centers. Locate the sink at the center of the work triangle, between the range and refrigerator.

The other primary components of the cleanup center are the garbage disposal and dishwasher. The dishwasher should be placed next to the sink to minimize drips on the floor. It should be to the left of the sink if the main cook is right-handed, and to the right if that person is left-handed.

You can store your everyday dishes, glassware, and utensils near the dishwasher for easy unloading, but you may prefer another convenient location, such as near the dining table.

If your plans include a trash compactor, have it installed on the side of the sink opposite the dishwasher to save steps

The cleanup center also requires ample storage for dish towels, cleaning products, and a garbage can. It's an ideal spot for a recycling system.

RIGHT: **A dishwasher is to the left and to the right, *not shown*, of two single-bowl stainless-steel sinks in this kitchen of a private chef and menu consultant. The 21-inch-wide sinks are 10 inches deep to accommodate large pots and pans.**

ABOVE: A cleanup center housing a double-bowl sink and dishwasher is located in the island of this kitchen. The location is handy for cleaning up after meals eaten at the island. The sink placement forms a tight work triangle with the range behind the island and the refrigerator, *not shown.*

Though not a typical kitchen work zone, a desk that can serve as a dedicated planning, homework, bill-paying, and organization area at the perimeter of the kitchen keeps the central work area clear of clutter and helps you manage your home efficiently. Include, at minimum, a small desk or work surface, chair, and filing drawer. If necessary, in addition to electrical outlets, plan for proper phone and computer connections.

Just as you would with the rest of your kitchen, take stock of all the items—paper, scissors, computer, stamps, file folders, letters, stationery, cards, markers, crafting supplies, wrapping paper—you might use in this space, and plan appropriate storage.

If your kitchen opens to adjoining rooms, tuck the work area in between the two spaces as part of the transition. Or consider annexing a portion of an underused butler's pantry for a desk area. If the area will serve as a play or homework zone for young children, take care to position it well out of the kitchen work zone but within view of the person preparing meals.

OPPOSITE: **Choose a smaller computer and install the printer in the pantry (with the cable behind the wall) to help keep the planning area from intruding into the kitchen.**

ABOVE RIGHT: **Outfit a work area as appropriate for your needs. Keep the design consistent with the rest of the kitchen.**

RIGHT: **Tuck in a built-in desk to maximize workspace in a small area. The adjacent closed cabinet conceals a printer and other supplies.**

organization
strategies

Much of a kitchen is devoted to organization. After all, cabinets account for much of the square footage and budget in a kitchen. But that does not guarantee an organized kitchen. To keep things neat and tidy, it's important to make putting something away as easy as leaving it out on the counter.

That said, you don't need to keep everything behind closed doors to be organized. Open shelving and hanging racks such as those seen in professional kitchens are being used in homes today. The overall concept is to save time, space, and money while simplifying your life.

TAKE INVENTORY

To have enough room, you need to get rid of what you never use. Before you plan for storage, decide what you really need to store. Sort through everything in your kitchen. Check out those cans and

OPPOSITE: Design storage to best meet your needs. Here, items such as pots, pans, knives, and dishes are stored out in the open where they are easily visible and accessible.

LEFT: Disguise a spice rack as an ordinary drawer. Use a pinch of this and a dash of that, then press the shelf back into its hiding place. Spices stay fresh; the kitchen stays neat.

ABOVE: A slice of kitchen storage can go incognito as an architectural element. This column slides out to reveal a mini pantry.

bottles at the back of the pantry and throw out what you never use or don't like. Toss out items that have expired and start out fresh. Pull out all of the items that have worked their way to the back of drawers. Toss broken items; assess the

Designer Tip

Plan wine storage in a place with minimal exposure to heat and light. If you're serious about wine and plan to collect and store bottles, consider a wine cooler. Otherwise, kitchen-rack storage is fine.

rest. If you didn't even know it was missing, chances are you won't use it again. Donate anything in good condition or have a garage sale.

Look out for duplicates. Some are worth keeping. When you're cooking

OPPOSITE: Here, space under an island is put to good use as a storage shelf for cookbooks and preserves.

ABOVE: Prevent bills, paperwork, and other necessities of managing your home from overtaking the kitchen. Carve out a nook in the corner for a work area. Small cubbies neatly contain and organize paper-

work and envelopes. A corkboard allows simple posting of daily events, phone messages, and family notes.

LEFT: Roll-out pantry cabinets store a plethora of canned and boxed staples in a compact area. Look for quality construction.

BELOW LEFT: Full-extension roll-out drawers are convenient for base cabinets, allowing easy access to items at the back. A pegboard base and adjustable dowel inserts enable you to efficiently stack plates, bowls and cups.

OPPOSITE: Cabinetmakers now offer more specialty storage inserts than ever to meet almost every organization need. Make use of narrow spaces with inserts such as these utensil holders.

Designer Tip

Store dry goods, such as cereal, pasta, rice, and beans, in airtight, see-through containers so you can gauge how much you have on hand.

---

dinner for a holiday crowd, it's good to have multiple serving dishes, spoons, and platters—and worth storing for that purpose. But other duplicates are just cluttering cabinets.

CREATE A STORAGE PLAN

Once you've pared down to what you really want and need, make a detailed list of what you have to store in the kitchen. That will allow you to design a space to best meet your needs. Here's how.

Designate a specific place for every thing. You'll be more likely to put things back where they belong and less likely to unknowingly duplicate items if you know exactly where things go.

Store it where you use it. Whenever possible, store items right where they are used. For example, store your mixer in an appliance garage in the baking center, where you can keep it plugged in and ready to use. Store your scrub brush and dish detergent close enough to

LEFT: Drawers installed in what is traditionally wasted toe-kick space maximize storage for pantry items.

BELOW: A shallow drawer is ideal for containing linens.

OPPOSITE: Positioning wines and spices away from the cooking center prolongs their lives. Both can be adversely affected by long exposure to high temperatures.

the sink that you can grab them without even looking up or taking a step.

Assign spaces based on frequency of use. Do you have more than one set of dishes? Store those used only at the holidays separate from those used for everyday meals.

Don't forget the waste. Though it may sound silly, you will need to store garbage and recyclables in your kitchen for short periods. Locate a recycling center close to the cleanup center and an exterior door, if possible, to make cleanup easy and for quick totes outside.

Keep it simple. When you have to open a door, stoop down, and reach to the back of a base cabinet to get something you use every day, chances are you won't take the time to put it away. Store the items you use frequently in the most convenient locations.

Make it comfortable. It is easier on your back to reach into a drawer and grab a utensil than it is to bend down and pull one out of the back of a base cabinet. Small drawers, however, may hold only a few small items. Consider installing pullouts in cabinets. For safety purposes, store heavier items in lower spots and lighter items in higher ones.

Put wasted space to work. Equip false sink fronts with pull-down baskets to hold scrub brushes and other small items. Narrow cabinets that would otherwise be filled with dead space can instead be fitted with spice racks. Install a lazy Susan to minimize wasted corner space.

Know your preference. If you like things within view, plan for open storage. Install standard base cabinets, but opt for open shelves rather than wall cabinets. Look for magnetic strips to stow knives near food prep areas. Hang pots from hooks on ceiling-mount racks. Just make sure you have plenty of head room.

If you prefer a sleek, behind-closed-doors approach to storage, install pullout racks, drawers, and tambour doors. To prevent utensils from becoming jumbled in drawers, use dividers or purchase upgraded drawers with these features built in.

Commit to a clutter-free kitchen. Once you have your belongings in your cabinets, you'll have to work to keep the new system in place. Don't fill every single spot; keep a few drawers open for new items. If storage space is limited, follow this rule: For every new thing that comes in, one old thing goes out.

ABOVE: A lift-up stand that supports a heavy mixer pulls double duty as storage and workstation. When not in use, the shelf unlocks and swings out of the way under the cabinet. The shelf below stows mixing bowls and mixer accessories.

ABOVE RIGHT: If your plans include a convenient pop-out toaster shelf, make sure it doesn't intrude into a main passageway.

RIGHT: These divided drawers keep pots, pans, and lids separated and out of sight. When you need them, both are right at hand when cooking on the range above. Use full-extension drawer slides rated to support at least 100 pounds.

ABOVE: Hanging racks keeps linens unwrinkled. When possible, position linen storage conveniently near the dining area.

ABOVE LEFT: A compact recycling center provides space for cans, bottles, and newspapers. Various configurations are available. Choose one that fits the space and has the necessary dividers to meet the recycling specifications of your community.

LEFT: This pullout baking center serves as a food preparation station when rolled out, and as storage when tucked under the countertop. Look for a rolling cart with lockable wheels and sturdy shelves—many can support 250 pounds or more.

LEFT: Vertical plate racks instill country charm and protect more delicate ceramic plates from chipping that can occur when dishes are stacked.

ABOVE: Glass shelves present an elegant twist on the open shelves found in most commercial-style kitchens.

BELOW: Tambour doors conceal small appliances when not in use. Electrical outlets, *not shown*, installed on the wall at the back of the storage area make it convenient to use the items without moving them far from storage.

easy cleaning

Visions of high style, not low maintenance, drive kitchen projects. However, unless you plan to make your newly remodeled kitchen purely for show and not for dough (the kind you roll out), be realistic: It's going to get dirty. To minimize the mess, consider these features at the design stage to prevent your dream kitchen from becoming a cleaning nightmare.

A TIGHT TRIANGLE
A good work triangle—the arrangement of the cooktop, sink, and refrigerator—minimizes the distance you have to carry things. It's the carrying that often leads to spills. One architect calls the area between workstations "drip space," so she puts the cooktop and sink close together. A center island can often compensate for a poor work triangle. If your kitchen is too small for a permanent island, a rolling cart or table can serve the same purpose.

FLOWING FLOORS
Thanks to gravity, most dirt ends up on the floor. Nothing will save you from regular cleaning, but the fewer seams and gaps in your floor, the fewer places dirt collects. The dirtiest place in any kitchen is the seam between the vertical surface of the toe-kick and the horizontal surface of the floor. That can be eliminated by "rolling" the edge of the floor up to the toe-kick, replacing the right-angle joint with a smooth curve. This technique is easiest with vinyl, linoleum, and tile, but it's also possible with wood if you have the edge pieces custom-milled.

Ceramic tile flooring is beautiful but needs constant attention. It obligates you to a daily sweeping. To make tile look cleaner, use large squares with narrow grout lines.

ABOVE: **A double sink set into a marble countertop makes cleanup a breeze.**

OPPOSITE: **Stainless-steel countertops and sinks—particularly when installed without seams that trap dirt—are easy to maintain.**

When you do have to clean the kitchen floor, technology can make the job easier. Consider a central vacuum system with an automatic dustpan inlet that installs in the baseboard or cabinetry toe-kick. You simply sweep dirt from the floor into the opening, and it gets sucked into a vacuum bag.

Countertop Containment.
Generally, the smoother the surface of your countertop and the fewer the seams, nooks, and crannies, the better. Curving your countertop up the wall creates a seamless backsplash that eliminates the dirt-catching right-angle joint where the counter meets the wall. In front, make sure the countertop edge overhangs the cabinet doors or drawers somewhat. Otherwise spills may get into cabinets or seep into drawers.

FULL ENCLOSURE
Handy receptacles for kitchen trash ease cleanup. Food scraps can go down the disposal, but you need a place for food packaging as well. If you live in a community with a recycling program, use different containers to sort paper, plastic, cardboard, and glass from nonrecyclable items. Sort as you work in the kitchen and you'll save a step on garbage day.

In addition to your trash, put away your treasures. Open shelves provide flexible storage, but they gather dust easily. Full or partial glass doors or display cases can block out much of the dust without blocking views of what's inside. Keep in mind that this creates a different cleaning chore: You have to clean the glass.

GRIME-FIGHTING CABINETS
Cabinets that have flat doors with a baked-on finish are easiest to clean. Painted cabinets with a high-gloss finish show dirt, but they're easy to wipe down.

Stained cabinets with a flatter or no-gloss finish don't show dirt as much, but they're more easily marred and harder to touch up. Raised-panel doors and elaborate molding around cabinetry look nice, but they are more difficult to clean.

When your fingers are greasy, pulls and handles keep the mess off the cabinetry surfaces. Look for hardware that makes it easy to open doors and drawers or you'll swap cleaning doors for cleaning handles. Three-inch-long metal pulls work nicely because you can open the door or drawer with one finger.

Cabinet and drawer inserts can also assist with cleanup. Some drawers, for example, have acrylic utensil liners that can be thrown right into the dishwasher.

COUNTER-SINK CONNECTION

How your sink is attached to the countertop affects ease of cleaning. Undermount sinks make it easy to wipe messes from the counter right into the sink. Self-rimming sinks, by contrast, have a perimeter lip that's sealed with a bead of caulk and can collect dirt. Perhaps the best solution is an integral sink in which the bowl and surrounding counter are one large piece of the same material, typically solid-surfacing or stainless steel. The lack of seams between the sink and countertop means there's nowhere for dirt to collect.

If an integral sink is too expensive, there's a cheaper solution: Buy a cutting board. After working, simply slide the cuttings from the board into the sink

The area behind the sink can be a trouble spot too. Most configurations leave about an inch between the edge of the sink and the backsplash. It's a gap just wide enough to attract dirt but too narrow to clean easily. You can solve the problem by making the sink countertop 1½ inches deeper. To accomplish this, 2×4s are placed between standard 24-inch-deep base cabinets and the wall. With the counter 25½ inches deep, a sponge or rag can easily wipe the space behind the sink.

ABLE APPLIANCES

Self-cleaning ovens, frost-free freezers, refrigerators with spill-catching shelves, and dishwashers with many cycles all help cut down on kitchen cleanup chores. If you've ever had to wash dirty drip pans from a stove top with conventional burners, you'll appreciate cooktops with smooth, ceramic surfaces. Even sealed gas burners with grates over the top are a cinch to clean.

Grease and smoke from cooking are common culprits in dirty kitchens, but a properly sized exhaust fan can help reduce greasy buildup on surfaces.

Built-in appliances eliminate common dirt traps, such as the space behind the refrigerator or openings between a freestanding range and the adjacent countertops.

OPPOSITE: **Flat-front cabinets with simple pulls are the easiest to clean. Fully enclosed cabinets throughout this kitchen minimize places for dust to collect.**

LEFT: **A well-equipped cleanup center makes kitchen duty less of a chore. Here, a double-drawer dishwasher, large sink, and compactor are grouped near the cooking center.**

elevations
and floor plans

When you or your kitchen professional completes a basic kitchen design that you like, it's time for a final detailed floor plan that includes the positions of all cabinets, appliances, fixtures, and utility connections. A well-marked plan will go a long way toward preventing time- and money-consuming changes during the actual remodeling process.

A floor plan is the overhead view of an architectural plan—what you'd see if you lifted the roof and looked down on the space.

An elevation view is the wall view of a space, what you'd see—from floor to ceiling—if you stood across from a wall.

A floor plan gives you a good idea of how a layout occupies space. An elevation lets you see how the kitchen is going to look to the human eye—the arrangement of doors and drawers, how wall and base cabinets relate to each other, how appliances function in a work triangle. An elevation takes in one wall at a time and—like the floor plan—shows the cabinets, appliances, fixtures, and outlets.

BELOW: An elevation view lets you get a sneak peek at what your kitchen will look like from your perspective as you stand in it when it's complete. Look at the elevation of your kitchen remodeling plan for problem areas such as where a drawer may collide with another drawer, cabinet door, or appliance when it is open.

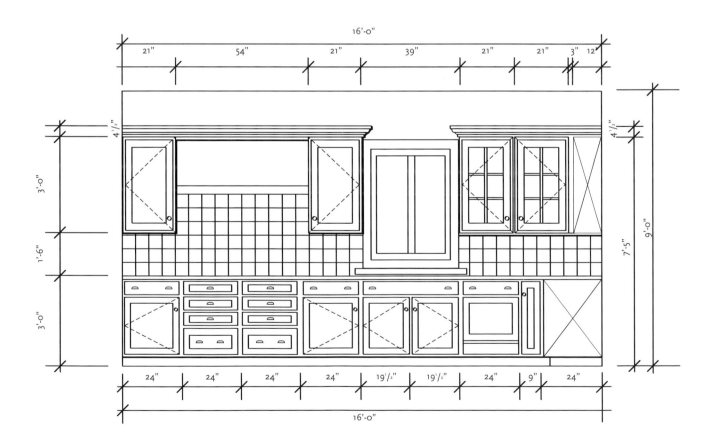

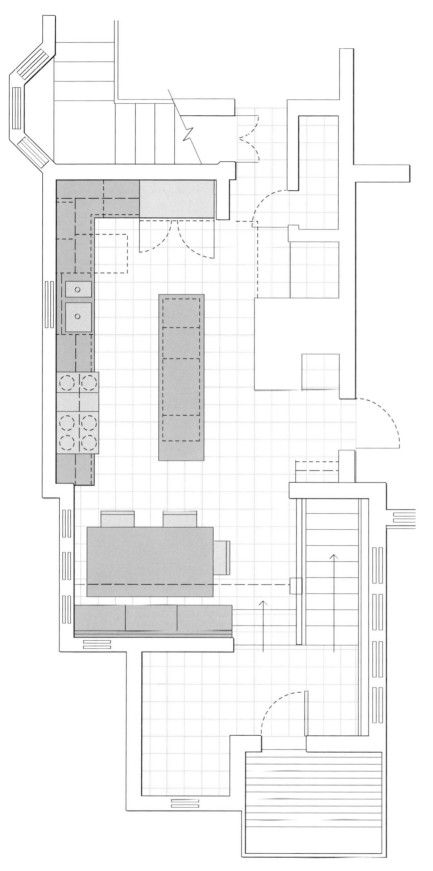

LEFT: A floor plan gives you a bird's-eye view of all the major elements in the kitchen: walls; windows; appliances such as the cooktop, sink, and refrigerator; closets; dining areas; and both wall and base cabinets. Base cabinets and countertops are represented by a solid line around the perimeter of the room, wall cabinets by a dotted line.

your final design
checklist

OPPOSITE: **Especially in a small kitchen, one of the most important questions is whether you will have enough storage space. There is no shortage of it in this kitchen, where base and wall cabinets are strategically placed and open shelves use space around the vent hood.**

ABOVE: **On the final run-through of your kitchen plan, make sure you have attended to the details that make the difference between a functional kitchen and a truly stunning upgrade. Here, subtle textures and colors highlight the backsplash.**

Spare yourself some hassle and headache by checking your kitchen's final design plan against this checklist of frequently overlooked points before ordering materials and beinning work.

Is there plenty of counterspace between appliances and sinks?

Is there enough space in kitchen corners to open drawers and doors fully?

Have you planned adjustable, roll-out, and vertical storage for the cabinets?

Do the cabinets come with handles or pulls?

Where will the pulls be placed on the cabinets? Will their design interfere with nearby appliance, door, or drawer openings?

Is the microwave oven at the right height for pulling out hot items? Can children use it safely?

Have you planned sufficient under-cabinet lighting?

Are light fixtures planned for above the sink, cooktop, or range?

Has the location of switch controls for lighting been planned?

Has the toe-kick below the cabinets been designed for the thickness of your flooring?

Will the new kitchen floor match

the style and height of flooring in adjoining rooms? How will it be joined?

Will new walls be trimmed with baseboard or molding at the floor?

Will this baseboard or cove meet the molding around the doors?

How will the walls be finished? Will they have to be prepared for painting or wallpaper?

How will the wall and ceiling finishes meet?

Do you have plenty of electrical outlets? If you're planning an island or a peninsula, don't forget outlets there too.

DOUBLE-CHECK YOUR PLAN

Is the work flow uninterrupted? Traffic should go around the kitchen's work triangle(s)—not through it. Likewise, special zones such as drink and snack centers shouldn't cross the work triangle. Otherwise collisions are likely.

Is there space between work zones? It's best to allow 4 to 6 feet between the sink and the range, 4 to 7 feet between the refrigerator and sink, and 4 to 9 feet between the range and refrigerator. Total space between all three points on the triangle should add up to no more than 26 feet. More than this standard can make kitchen work inefficient and tiring. Remember, too, that for all but zealous baking enthusiasts, ovens can be placed outside the work triangle.

ABOVE LEFT: **Details make all the difference. A pullout shelf brings cutting boards and pans out into the open for a family that enjoys frequent baking. In your final design check, make sure your family's special interests are represented.**

LEFT: **You may be eager to get on with construction, but taking the time to get all the details right—such as this slender spice cabinet—will ensure long-term enjoyment.**

Is there counter space near each work zone? For counter space on both sides of the sink, 18 to 24 inches is a must. You also need space near the refrigerator—at least 15 inches on the handle side—to set down food. Similarly essential is a heat-resistant 15- to 18-inch space on each side of a cooktop and on one side of a wall-mount oven for hot pans and supplies.

Do you have enough storage space where you need it? Basic storage standards suggest 18 square feet of cabinet space plus an additional ½ square foot for each family member. Keep items where they will be used: pots near the range, food near the main prep area. You'll need cool storage too: 12 cubic feet of refrigerator-freezer combo for two people, plus 2 cubic feet for each additional family member. You needn't store everything within an arm's reach. Infrequently used equipment and specialty foods can be kept in a pantry closet near the kitchen.

Last but not least, will you enjoy your kitchen? Whether you're reviving your kitchen or giving it a to-the-studs makeover, the time and money you put into the project should result in a space that you enjoy immensely. So if you're excited about your plans, forge ahead. But if parts of your kitchen plan nag at you, go back and review them, looking for alternatives. If you've done the planning yourself, get a pro's opinion; if you've been working with someone, seek another opinion.

A Good Fit. Make certain that your appliances and cabinetry will fit together before you order either. For each appliance that you'll be using, get the manufacturer's specifications and check them against your cabinet specifications. Always double-check manufacturers' specifications for appliances. For instance, heights for appliance drawers for warming, refrigeration, and dishwashing vary by manufacturer.

ABOVE: A convenient swing-arm pot-filler faucet above the range eliminates the hassle of carrying heavy, sloshing pots of water from the main sink but requires additional plumbing expenses.

express yourself

Personalize with color, art, accessories—whatever makes the heart of the home uniquely yours. »

>> All visual arts are subject to the vagaries of fashion. One kitchen trend that doesn't seem to be going away is the use of natural elements, such as wood, stone, and metal. Colors that complement these materials also remain strong in the design world—especially the spice tones of paprika, mustard, cinnamon, oregano, and sage. What could be a more appropriate palette for the kitchen?

color trends

Colors rise and fall in popularity and are subject to personal preference. Some color schemes, however, have stood the test of time. The most classic is the all-white kitchen.

Often accented with one color, such as blue, white is a popular choice for the kitchen because it's clean-looking and helps visually downplay dirty dishes and pots-and-pans clutter. The only downside of an all-white kitchen is that it can look sterile and cold, but that's easily fixed with the addition of warm-toned elements, such as a honey-color wood floor, or soft accents, such as curtains at the windows or an upholstered banquette seat.

Even an all-white kitchen has color in it: An oak floor infuses it with yellow; a granite countertop can be gray, pink, green, or black. Keep in mind, too, that there are hundreds of whites; white can be warm or cool—it can even be hot.

True colors—as opposed to white, which is neutral—are generally considered warm or cool. Warm colors, such as tones of red, yellow, and orange, are energizing. Cool colors, such as blue, green, and violet, are calming. Color does indeed affect mood. Studies have shown that exposure to red, for instance,

Pleasing Patterns. Because the kitchen is a busy place with lots going on visually, it's generally a good idea to use pattern fairly sparingly and to keep what is used clean and simple. Geometrics, such as checks (think of the classic checkerboard floor), ginghams, stripes, and plaids, are always good choices, as are airy florals and classics, such as Provençal-style prints and toiles.

Natural materials, such as wood and stone (and fabricated materials that mimic natural materials, such as laminate and some solid-surfacing), have patterns of their own that are generally subtle and will blend with nearly any other pattern.

quickens the pulse and breathing rate and increases the appetite. Any color can be used with great success in the kitchen if you follow a few color guidelines.

Generally, it is wise to pick one base color and then one or two accent colors. Complementary colors—those that sit opposite one another on the color wheel—intensify each other and impart energy Analogous colors—those that sit next to one another on the color wheel—are visually softer together and will make a space seem more serene. Neutrals, such as taupe, tan, black, white,

cream, and gray, can be a color scheme in and of themselves or can be paired with nearly any other color.

When thinking about what kind of color scheme you'd like for your kitchen, keep in mind the hues that run through a favorite quilt, inherited willowware dishes from your grandmother, or a beloved painting. Perhaps your color inspiration will come from the walls of a villa you visited in Tuscany, an adobe home you admired in Mexico, or a cottage garden you strolled through in England. Choose a color scheme based

on something you love and you'll never tire of it.

OPPOSITE: The citrus green that distinguishes these cabinets is actually two shades. The lower cabinets are darker than the upper ones and the tall pantry.

ABOVE: After a period of fairly neutral options, color is showing up again in kitchen appliances. Pair a peacock-blue range with natural cabinets. Add subtle blue accents throughout the room.

furnishings

After cabinetry the primary furnishings in a kitchen are the pieces that compose the dining arrangement. A peninsula or an island for casual meals begs for casual seating: barstools, either round or square, with or without backs and seat cushions. If you have the space and inclination, a kitchen table is more comfortable for eating because you don't have to climb up into the chair and you can face your dining companions.

Let the style you've chosen for your kitchen guide you in picking an appropriate dining set. Perhaps it's a 1950s-style laminate table with easy-wipe vinyl-padded chairs, or maybe it's a marble-topped table with Italian-country-style ladderback chairs fitted with rush seats. Mix a distressed pine table with painted chairs—or use an eclectic mix of one-of-a-kind chairs you've discovered at antiques shops and tag sales.

There is no rule that says you must march out and buy a brand-new dinette set with matching table and chairs when you update a kitchen. If that's what pleases you, by all means do it. But dining furniture creates an intimate space for eating and conversing with family and friends; it should speak volumes about who you are. What you already have may be ideal.

BANQUETTES AND BOOTH SEATS
Coming in all shapes and styles, booth seats and banquettes strike our fancy for the same reasons we choose a booth instead of a table at a restaurant: privacy, intimacy, camaraderie, even romance. If you've ever dined at a table in the middle of a crowded restaurant, you know the uneasy feeling of being "on

stage." In that same setting, a booth lets you forget your surroundings and focus on your dining companions.

Although privacy isn't a concern in your own kitchen, a charming banquette does inspire the same kind of physical closeness and sense of fun and fellowship you experience when dining out. Booth seating begs an informal atmosphere, inviting us to spread out (or squeeze together), put our elbows on the table, and just enjoy the meal.

If carefully placed and designed, a banquette does even more, making the most of precious kitchen floor space,

providing convenient storage above and below the seats, and saving time and energy in serving meals. Why run yourself ragged going back and forth between the kitchen and the dining room when a banquette puts the table just a few steps from the stove?

ABOVE: **Peninsulas provide ideal seating for two in small or galley kitchens where there is no space for an island.**

OPPOSITE: **In an eat-in kitchen, mix wood species, stains, and painted furniture for a more interesting look.**

In a larger kitchen, booth seats can be a miniature dining room, a haven separate from the work area. In a smaller space, even an alcove, window, or wasted corner can be the perfect spot to squeeze in seating for four. Because you don't have to pull out any chairs, you don't need as much clearance for a banquette as you do for a traditional table. Less chair sliding gives your floor a break, too. From a style standpoint, box seats add warmth and personality to your kitchen with the colors and materials you choose for the cushions, eating surface, surrounding walls, and window treatments.

As an integral part of the room's design, a banquette is a constant reminder that your kitchen isn't just for cooking—it's also for eating.

BEYOND THE KITCHEN TABLE

If you want to create the furnished, unfitted look that is so popular today, consider limiting the number of built-in base and wall cabinets and substituting one-of-a-kind pieces, such as an old armoire or buffet for storing dishes, cookware, and foodstuffs. It can be retrofitted with either stationary or pull-out shelving to make it more efficient and functional for the modern kitchen. Mix painted pieces with wood, metal, or

Designer Tip

Some islands serve as seating for casual meals, some purely as work surfaces and storage. Some are stationary; others can be brought in rather than built in. Some technically peninsulas or extensions of the countertop. Nearly anything with a virtually indestructible food-safe surface that's at a comfortable height for food prep and eating can serve as an island: an antique stove fitted with a countertop, a rustic pine farm table, a mahogany library table, or a marble-top baker's table.

laminate. Consider a freestanding bookshelf for your cookbook collection, and include a comfortable chair for reading, planning menus, or taking a rest.

A caveat: The kitchen, with its inevitable grease, steam, drips, and spills, is not the ideal place to use upholstered furniture with abandon. If you want upholstery in the kitchen, use it sparingly, be sure fabrics have been treated to resist stains, and take care that the material is easy to clean. Machine-washable slipcovers for dining chairs are one option to consider.

Banquette Basics. Besides the standard restaurant booth setup, banquette options include U-shapes, L-shapes, semicircles, and hybrids combining bench seats and chairs. Although box seats work especially well in recessed areas, you can build one flush against the wall too. A booth for four with fixed seating can fit into a 42×60-inch space. Here are other considerations:

Standard table height and width is 30 inches. Allow 12 inches from the top of the benches to the table surface; benches should be 18 inches high. Let the table overlap the benches by 3 or 4 inches on each side. For more legroom, set the benches back a few inches and add a "heel kick" on the floor below the table overlap.

Allow a minimum of 21 inches of table and seating length per person. Also allow for 18 inches of seating depth, not counting the back support.

Allow 54 inches for each leg of the U and 78 inches for the rear bench. U-shapes need more generous dimensions to avoid knee-squeezing corners.

Leave plenty of vertical clearance for a hanging light fixture. Bumped heads can result if a fixture is placed too low over a booth.

ABOVE: **Outfit a banquette with a bench on one side and chairs on the other for more flexibility than two benches offer.**

OPPOSITE: **Even in a formal-style kitchen, the option to pull up stools to an island for a quick bite to eat is a nice alternative to a full sit-down meal.**

window treatments

Banks of cabinetry, long stretches of countertop, and boxy appliances combine to make your kitchen appear angular and sharp. The visual and textural softness of fabric is an ideal way to filter harsh light into a soft glow and break up the straight lines of windows.

To choose fabric, pull colors from the rest of the materials used in the kitchen. Granite or solid-surfacing countertops, for instance, are often flecked with several hues. Patterned rugs and wallpaper also offer many color choices.

Whether you opt for a solid color or patterned window treatment depends on how much visual stimulation is going on in the rest of the room. If a granite, marble, or solid-surfacing countertop has an elaborate (if random) design, it can clash with a busy curtain pattern, so stick to solid colors. If your backsplash has an intricate scheme, or if your cabinets are painted or stained with more than one shade, choose fabric with a simple, complementary pattern.

Remember that some fabrics work better in the kitchen than others. If there's a sink nearby, don't go with a fabric that might stain or run if it's splashed with water or soapsuds (silk, for instance, is notorious for staining). If you'd like the treatment to block an unpleasant view, a dark or heavy fabric will do the trick. Lace or other loosely woven fabric, such as gauze or scrim, will obscure views but let in light. Never hang curtains above a cooktop or range.

Think, too, about the practical applications of your window dressings. If blinding light beams through the window just as you're fixing dinner, you'll want to use a shade or heavier fabric, but include a tieback for the curtains so you can enjoy the light when you're not standing by the window.

If you'd like some privacy while still basking in the sunshine, consider installing café curtains; they'll block the view from the bottom half of the window but leave the top half clear. If privacy is not an issue and you're fortunate enough to have a great view of gardens or the backyard from the window, mount the treatment up and out of the way so that it's merely decorative.

ABOVE: Rich tan-and-black plaid silk curtains help make this kitchen warm and inviting.

LEFT: Casual blinds can be lowered to shield the breakfast area from glaring light as necessary.

OPPOSITE: Shades that can be raised from the top or the bottom offer flexible lighting and viewing options in a breakfast area with windows on two sides.

art and
accessories

A truly successful kitchen does more than function well; it has personality. Accessories, artwork, and treasures of all kinds are what give a room its unique character. In composing a kitchen style, don't stop designing after the cabinets, countertops, and appliances have been selected. Nudge your imagination into action, and treat your kitchen as an artist's canvas.

Don't banish artwork to more traditional display areas. Instead, look around your house for design ideas to bring into the kitchen. Framed prints can embellish carefully selected colors, fabrics, and surface materials throughout the kitchen. Small paintings might adorn a soffit. Larger pieces can enhance dining area walls. If framed prints seem too typical, consider a mural to spark conversation.

LITTLE THINGS COUNT

Often, it's the small touches that have the greatest effect on a decorating scheme. Because accessories are the most personal part of decorating, they should be chosen and displayed with care. Accent items should reflect your personality. Accessories don't have to be one-of-a-kind. If an item has meaning for you, it's worthy of attention.

Don't be shy about showing off your treasures. Beautiful dishes, mementos, heirlooms, or trinkets encourage guests to linger while the host cooks or cleans.

ABOVE LEFT: Make use of the things you love. These light fixtures are made from old frosted German milk bottles.

LEFT: Colorful reproduction bowls make a beautiful backdrop that can be drawn from when a serving bowl is needed.

Glass-front, china, and armoirelike cabinets are perfect for displaying collections. Spaces above cabinets also offer room for displays. Almost any collection can find a home in the kitchen. When arranging objects, keep scale and balance in mind and don't overcrowd. To call attention to your collection, especially at night, consider spotlights or specially designed display lights.

WHERE TO START

Go on a treasure hunt in your own house. Chances are, you'll come across an interesting object. Once you're sure you've unearthed all your home's hidden treasures, visit art galleries, antiques stores, and accessories shops. You'll develop a discerning eye. Experiment with arrangements; rotate things into the kitchen from other rooms. Vignettes are small scenes in a large setting, islands of beauty to behold. Countertops and other surfaces are candidates for vignettes. The idea is to create a composition that invites viewing and stirs interest, even if just in passing.

BELOW: **Extend the opening between the kitchen and dining room, build a room divider in the center, and transform the side facing the dining room table into an art display wall.**

ABOVE: **Vintage pottery, kitchenware, knickknacks, and other flea-market finds create inexpensive charm.**

7 realize your dreams

Achieving a kitchen that meets your goals within your budget isn't easy. Design professionals can help. »

>> Brace yourself. When it comes to remodeling your kitchen, you'll inevitably part with more money than you expect to spend. Balancing your dreams with financial realities is a complex game of give-and-take, one that demands research and creativity to master. But if you plan wisely and take a few tips from the pros, your next kitchen will not only be a good investment, it will also pay off in unexpected ways.

calculating costs

HOW MUCH SHOULD YOU SPEND?

Real estate agents agree that you can invest 10 to 15 percent of your home's total value in remodeling a kitchen and expect to recoup a significant portion when you sell the house—anywhere from 50 to 120 percent. In the hottest housing markets, the accepted ratio of the kitchen remodeling cost to a home's overall value can climb as high as 25 percent.

The only way to assess the value of your own investment is to match your precise plans and budgets with local market conditions. If you own a $150,000 house with chipped laminate counters and invest $12,000 in a six-burner professional-style range but little else, you won't see much of a return. Talk to real estate agents who understand local values, tastes, and trends—not just in your area, but also in your specific neighborhood.

You should research financing options too. Unlike a loan for a $35,000 car, the interest on a home equity loan is tax deductible. In a competitive lending market, you might turn around and refinance your entire mortgage when the work is done. Considering that a new car declines in value the moment you leave the lot, and a new kitchen holds its value much longer, the investment potential is clear.

ABOVE: **Just as with car buyers, kitchen outfitters suffer sticker shock. Plan carefully; appliances, cabinets, flooring, labor, installation, and design costs add up quickly.**

WHAT COULD YOU SPEND?

Though we realize it's possible to spend $100,000 on a kitchen, we still like to imagine luxuries in our kitchen for a finished price of $25,000. That may not be realistic. According to the National Kitchen and Bath Association, the average professionally designed American kitchen remodeling project in 1998 had a price tag of nearly $27,000, including management and labor costs. Most of those kitchens were at least 11×14 feet, and cabinets accounted for roughly half of the total expense. But very few included high-ticket items such as granite or solid-surfacing countertops

and large, commercial-style appliances.

To put costs into perspective, we've identified three general categories of remodeling and what you can expect to achieve in each price range. Figures assume that you're not choosing rock-bottom materials, because you want the kitchen to last more than a year or two.

• **Modest project ($5,000–$15,000):** In this price range, you'll typically stay within the existing walls and make no significant changes to the layout. At the low end, you can paint or refurbish existing wood cabinets and replace most of the surfaces and fixtures (such as, the

ABOVE: **Older appliances stayed in this remodeled kitchen to make the budget work. The 15-year-old refrigerator looks new paneled to match the cherry cabinetry. The microwave oven has a built-in slot.**

sink and faucet and a light or two) with no-frills options. You also can swap out some appliances with economically priced models if you keep them in the same position so that no changes in wiring are necessary.

At the high end, you can choose better appliances and replace cabinets (but don't expect any custom sizes or finishes). To get quality in one area, you

should be prepared to make sacrifices in another—such as settling for laminate flooring or resilient flooring, forgetting about that snazzy cooktop, and doing some of the work yourself if you have the skills.

In any case, achieving good results with a modest budget depends largely on your ability to research and plan extensively. Expect to endure a lot more inconvenience than a homeowner who pays a seasoned professional to manage all the details.

• **Midrange project ($15,000–$45,000):** Even at $15,000, you can expect good-quality stock cabinets. Let the budget grow and you can opt for laminate counters with stylish edging and an entirely new suite of midrange appliances. Moreover, you can make some improvements to the layout—perhaps even opening the existing space to another room.

Beware, however, of potential budget busters that lurk in any wall you plan to remove. The extra demolition, carpentry, and finishing work alone can

easily add $1,000, even in a wall that isn't load bearing. And the total cost may be many times higher. What kind of surface damage to surrounding spaces will your remodeling cause? And what's inside those walls you're opening? Will you have to reroute plumbing, ducts, or electrical cables? Are the floors uneven between spaces, demanding an entirely new floor throughout? Will you need a specially engineered beam to support a load-bearing span? Those are the possible perils of just opening up the

space. If you're planning on expanding the kitchen into an adjacent area, you're likely to spend substantially more.

In its 2004 Cost vs. Value study, the trade magazine *Remodeling* pegged the average "midrange kitchen remodeling" at just above $42,000 (including contractor costs determined by R.S. Means, a leading publisher of national construction costs). For that price, a roughly 200 square foot kitchen acquired an improved layout with a 3×5-foot island, new semicustom cabinets (30 linear feet), new appliances (with a separate wall oven and cooktop), custom lighting, and nice laminate counters and resilient flooring. For many potential remodelers, that cost sounds prohibitive. But there's good news in the report too: The average amount recouped nationally through increased resale values for that midrange remodeling was 79.4 percent. That's approximately $33,000 of the remodeling money spent. And in home-sales hot spots, the return on investment can climb even higher. (Visit www.remodeling.hw.net for more information.)

• Deluxe project ($45,000 and up): Most designers will tell you that $45,000 or $50,000 will not buy you a truly "deluxe" kitchen. And they're right. That is a serious amount of money, but it takes a savvy, well-educated consumer—one who's willing to make some compromises and devote significant time to the project—to achieve high-end luxuries for "so little."

A bit of shopping reveals the cold facts. Do you have your heart set on a commercial-style range and fridge? Add the requisite vent hood, and the price tag could easily exceed $25,000 for these appliances alone. Add amenities such as wine chillers, extra ovens, and special drawers to keep veggies crisp and dinner warm, and you could be looking at a $35,000 appliance suite. Custom cabinets often command $500 or more per linear foot. So if you have even 30 linear feet of cabinets, that tab also runs at least $15,000. The budget is broken before you even begin to consider sought-after luxuries such as granite-slab countertops ($10,000 for a typical installation) and hardwood floors ($2,000–$5,000), not to mention design and construction costs.

WHAT WILL YOU SPEND?

Every kitchen job is highly individual. Costs vary depending on the materials you choose and the condition of your home. A homeowner who has old knob-and-tube wiring may end up spending as much as $5,000 to $7,000 just to update the plumbing and electrical systems. The cost of a simple addition runs about $150 per square foot or higher.

To estimate costs of your own project as accurately as possible, there's no substitute for a detailed plan. First, sketch the precise layout of your intended kitchen. You'll undoubtedly change things later, but to get a clear picture of costs, you have to start somewhere. Next, list every conceivable item you'll buy, and start shopping to estimate prices—fixture by fixture, cabinet by cabinet. (Cabinet prices per foot might be only half your true cost; they're based on a basic box.) There's no substitute for actually visiting local stores and showrooms to narrow your choices and get accurate figures.

After you've burned a little shoe leather, you can start refining your plan. Identify priorities and eliminate luxuries you can live without. This is a good time to consult with a designer and start soliciting bids for work: You have a good idea what things cost, you know what you intend to spend, and you know what you hope to achieve.

One final note: Even the most carefully planned project will have unforeseen costs, which often add 20 percent to a budget. If you don't have that wiggle room, create a simpler plan up front. You'll sleep better at night and will still enjoy your new kitchen in the morning.

LEFT: Deluxe kitchens are beautiful and expensive. This kitchen features cabinets that were crafted in England and then painted and antiqued on-site. The chandeliers were made in Italy and imported from England. Cutlery drawers are lined with leather. The limestone countertops, floors, and backsplashes are heated and treated to feel as hard as granite.

working with a designer

If you're enlisting the services of a professional kitchen designer, the success of your project depends on your working relationship. Here's how to find the right person—and the right level of service—for the job.

THE INTERVIEW

While you are interviewing designers for the job, they are probably "interviewing" you, too, to determine whether they can meet your requirements and budget.

If your initial discussions go well, a designer will likely conduct a more thorough survey of your needs, and your project will be underway. Be ready to answer or discuss these questions:

Are there other professionals involved in your project? It's common for homeowners to work with architects, interior designers, builders, and other professionals. The kitchen designer should contact them to open lines of communication. If you are not yet working with other professionals, the designer's firm may offer any or all of these services, either with in-house personnel or through its network of construction and design professionals.

What kind of kitchen do you envision? Whether you're remodeling a

ABOVE: A designer can open your mind to new possibilities for cabinetry styles and finishes, such as the painted beadboard door this designer is showing to clients.

RIGHT: Designer touches such as painted cabinet interiors hightlight display pieces.

OPPOSITE: Prior to meeting with a designer, create a scrapbook of style preferences. Ask your designer for additional recommendations based on your selections.

kitchen or building a new home, the designer needs to know how much planning you've done, as well as your style, color, and equipment preferences. Write down as much information as you can. The more preliminary information you provide, the closer the designer can come to your dream kitchen.

When do you plan to start and complete your project? Scheduling subcontractors is a key task. Some cabinetry may be ready for immediate delivery from local warehouses, whereas custom or semicustom cabinets may require up to 16 weeks. The designer will help establish a schedule, then work to meet the deadlines.

What is your budget? The kitchen designer needs to know your budget constraints to help maximize your dollar, evaluate the cost efficiency of products, and make effective trade-offs.

DESIGNER SERVICES

Kitchen designers generally offer three levels of service.

Level 1—Basic layout: Retailers such as lumberyards, home centers, and kitchen and bath distributors often offer computer generated images of your new kitchen for free. You are responsible for providing accurate measurements as well as for installing cabinets, appliances, and surfacing materials. You probably will not receive much customization or problem-solving expertise.

Level 2—Design strategies: Many retailers employ designers who can discuss your remodeling needs and preferences and offer suggestions. The designer will visit your home to take measurements and later present a floor plan and ideas. After analyzing the plan, you may request changes.

The designer may or may not handle installation. This level of service usually involves a fee, either a minimal measurement fee or design fee.

Level 3—Design and project management: At the highest level of service, your designer will work with you to oversee the project from start to finish. He or she will analyze the kitchen and adjoining areas, look for potential structural changes, and create working drawings for your inspection. Once the plans are finalized, the designer will order products and monitor the remodeling process.

This level is more typical of kitchen dealers, design firms, and remodelers.

FEE STRUCTURES

Fees vary depending on location and the designer's level of expertise.

Some designers require a retainer or consultation fee on their initial visit. It is most commonly an hourly fee, but it may be a percentage of the project's total estimated cost. Typically, this fee is not applied toward the cost of any products you buy through the designer or the designer's employer.

Designers who sell products may include the design fee in the cost of the project. If you don't proceed with the project, you will probably be charged for designer services.

PREPARING FOR YOUR FIRST VISIT

Before you meet with a designer, hone in on your style preferences by studying magazines, visiting with friends, and contemplating your family's lifestyle. Create a scrapbook of ideas by cutting out photos and circling the elements that catch your eye. Make notes about things you like and dislike, about the way your family lives in your kitchen and about suggestions you've received. Take these to your first meeting. The better prepared you are, the more likely it is you'll get exactly what you want. Include:

• Major structural changes needed.

• General style and color preferences.

• Cabinetry—style, color, wood type, and organizational features, such as bins for flatware, and pullout shelves.

• Appliances, sinks—style, color, functional features. Do you need a prep sink, two ovens, or dishwashers?

• Surfacing materials for countertops, flooring, and backsplashes.

• Number of cooks: What are the responsibilities of each? What appliances and equipment are required?

• Workstations: Do you want auxiliary workstations, such as a baking center, laundry area, or homework space?

• Planning area: How much desk space do you need? Do you want file drawers, bookshelves, or mail cubbies?

• Eating area: Would you prefer a full eat-in kitchen, a breakfast nook, or a snack counter?

• Social areas: Do you need seating for guests? A hospitality/beverage center, a TV area, or a snack station for children?

The lesson is a simple one: Know your priorities and limitations. That's the best way to ensure that a designer can deliver the kitchen you really want

working
with a contractor

When you plan a remodeling project, it's natural to consider what you want. But you must also know what your contractor will need to get the job done well. Your understanding of the planning, preparation, and construction process helps you communicate better and complete a successful project. Explore these ways you can assist your contractor.

BE CONSISTENT

Contractors appreciate clients who can communicate their vision clearly. Collect ideas and images from magazines and books. Present these examples to your contractor, and if you have details you are intent on including, mention them specifically.

Visually communicating ideas puts everyone on the same page. Clear communication translates into fewer surprises once work is under way. Changed orders or reconsidered decisions are a part of every remodeling effort, but they eat your money and your contractor's time.

BE REALISTIC ABOUT BUDGET

When planning with your contractor, be honest about your budget. If a few items push you over the top, it's likely your contractor can help you get the look you want for less by suggesting some alternative materials. Keep in mind, though, that price tags at the local home center may be lower than those quoted by your contractor. Sometimes this is due to standard markups on materials, but estimates may also reflect handling requirements and installation costs.

MIND YOUR MONEY MATTERS

The contract you sign will stipulate when payments are due. Plan to adhere to the dates without exception. Late payments will undoubtedly slow the process, especially if you're working with an independent remodeler who needs the payments to purchase your materials.

PREPARE THE SITE

Whether your kitchen project involves minor or major structural modifications, remove any obstacles to site access. Some contractors will move large items such as furniture without charge; others won't. Discuss your contractor's policy in advance. Remove all items of value from the space. Don't let pets get underfoot, and don't make workers responsible for preventing animals' escape through a doorway or wall opening.

EXPECT CHAOS

Remodeling is messy. Even under the best of circumstances, there's going to be stress. Discuss peacekeeping issues beforehand, including rules about smoking in the house, which bathroom to use, and where to park. Avoid the work zone as much as possible, for your safety and that of the workers. Children tend to be fascinated with the tools and big messes of remodeling. Arrange a few supervised visits to satisfy their curiosity, but make sure they are otherwise occupied and out of harm's way.

Observing these fundamental guidelines should promote mutual goodwill between you and your contractor. As in most business relationships, attitude can make all the difference. A contractor who sees that you respect his or her time and services is likely to reciprocate by respecting you and your home and delivering the quality you expect.

Designer Tip

Get bids from two or three contractors for your kitchen project, and get them in writing. Remember that price is not the only consideration; there are the issues of personality, quality, workmanship, and professionalism too. Ask for references from anyone who gives you a bid. You should speak both to recent clients and those from five to eight years ago. This way you can ask questions about how the contractor's work has held up.

Coping with a Kitchen Overhaul. From the time you contract
with your builder, discuss strategies for minimizing disruption to your home, family, and lifestyle. Some contractors will not start a project until everything on order has arrived; the old cabinets will not be removed, for example, until the new ones are in the warehouse. Careful timing of orders can save the family unnecessary discomfort. Here are a few more strategies for surviving the chaos of remodeling a kitchen.

- Set up a temporary kitchen. Create space for a microwave oven, countertop, and sink in the basement, laundry room, or extra bathroom.
- Use carpet runners and plastic partitions to minimize the impact of grime. Ask about limiting worker access into the home to one entrance.
- Outline your menus. Ask your contractor how long you'll be without the use of a kitchen and plan accordingly.
- Have a backup plan. Talk to friends and relatives and arrange an exchange of services: You bring the groceries, and everyone helps prepare a meal in their kitchen.
- Don't internalize stress. Picture yourself as a good person in a tough situation. Know your stress buttons and work to balance the tension when it becomes too much.
- Monitor your self-image. You know all of those TV commercials showing happy people living in spotless homes? Forget about them. Your home's condition during a remodeling project is not a reflection of your worth.

kitchen planning kit

To transform your kitchen dreams into reality, consider the details. Sketch out some ideas of your own, even if you will work with a kitchen planner or designer. Doing so is recommended because your drawings provide insight into what you're after. Use the kitchen planning kit on the following pages to work through the process.

To help you consider how you'll use your new kitchen, visualize the following: how traffic should flow, where you'd like the various work centers—food storage and prep, cooking, and cleanup—how you'll work in a home planning area, how the kitchen relates to the rooms around it, and whether you'd like to incorporate a gathering, snacking, or eating area into the room. Finally, consider which architectural features you'd like to add or highlight and what types, sizes, and styles of appliances, cabinetry, shelving, and furnishings you want to include.

Plot the space. Use the grids on page 158. One square equals 1 square foot of floor space. Plot your kitchen, including any pantry, entry, mudroom, office, dining area, or bump-outs you'd like to add or remodel at the same time. One of the keys to making your kitchen both functional and beautiful is good placement of doors, windows, appliances, cabinetry, islands, and built-in features.

Use architectural symbols, *right,* to mark the position of existing architectural features. Use a different color to indicate added features such as the placement of built-ins and furniture. Use dotted lines to mark obstructions, including prominent light fixtures and angled ceilings.

Use the templates to experiment with different placements for furniture, appliances, and built-in features. Trace or photocopy the appropriate items from the templates on the following pages and cut them out with a crafts knife or scissors. If you have furniture or special features such as a peninsula or island, measure and draw them to the same scale on the grid paper.

TEMPLATE TIME

Use these templates to mark the placement of common kitchen components. The templates include plan-view (top-down) perspectives, allowing you to create floor plans. Most kitchen components are represented here, including various types and sizes of drop-in and freestanding ranges, cooktops, grills, and refrigerators. Pay attention to details such as door swings and drawer extensions (marked in dotted lines on these templates) as you consider the placment of these items in the room. If you don't see a template for something you'd like to include, draw your own.

PLANNING GRID

Use a photocopier to reproduce the grid at its original size, then cut out the templates on pages 154 to 157 to design your kitchen. Grid scale: 1 square equals 1 square foot.

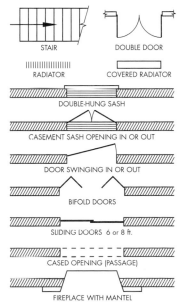

Wall Cabinets – Storage Angles
(Appliance Garage)

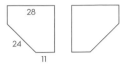

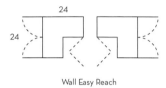

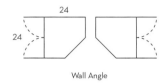

Standard Cabinet Height: 18 ½ inches.

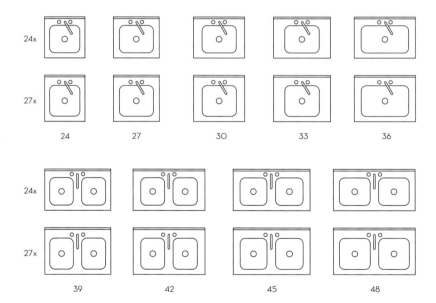

Wall Easy Reach

Wall Angle

Standard Cabinet Heights: 30, 36, and 42 inches.

Sink Bases

	24	27	30	33	36
24x					
27x					

	39	42	45	48
24x				
27x				

Wall Cabinets - Penninsula Wall Pieces

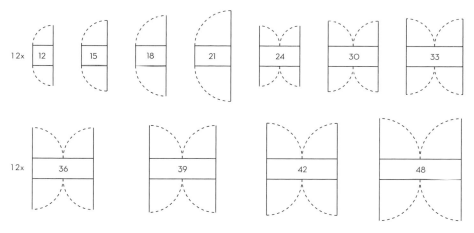

12x | 12 | 15 | 18 | 21 | 24 | 30 | 33

12x | 36 | 39 | 42 | 48

Standard Cabinet Heights: 23 1/2, 30, 36, 42, and 48 inches.

Wall Cabinets

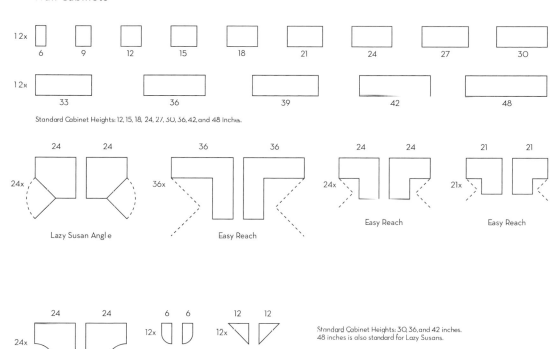

12x | 6 | 9 | 12 | 15 | 18 | 21 | 24 | 27 | 30

12x | 33 | 36 | 39 | 42 | 48

Standard Cabinet Heights: 12, 15, 18, 24, 27, 30, 36, 42, and 48 inches.

24 24
24x
Lazy Susan Angle

36 36
36x
Easy Reach

24 24
24x
Easy Reach

21 21
21x
Easy Reach

24 24
24x
Open Shelf with Curve

6 6
12x
Open Shelf End

12 12
12x
Wall Corner

Standard Cabinet Heights: 30, 36, and 42 inches.
48 inches is also standard for Lazy Susans.

Standard Cabinet Heights: 30, 36, and 42 inches.

Base Cabinets

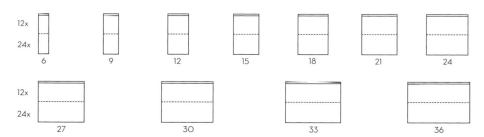

12x
24x | 6 | 9 | 12 | 15 | 18 | 21 | 24

12x
24x | 27 | 30 | 33 | 36

Standard Cabinet Heights: 34 1/2 inches.

Cooktops

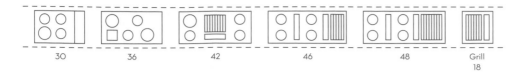

| 30 | 36 | 42 | 46 | 48 | Grill 18 |

Drop-In Ranges

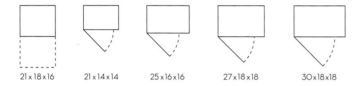

| 27 | 30 | 30 |

Freestanding Ranges

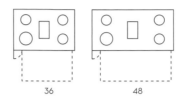

| 36 | 48 |

Microwave Ovens

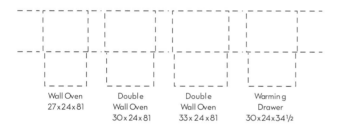

| 21x18x16 | 21x14x14 | 25x16x16 | 27x18x18 | 30x18x18 |

Wall Ovens

| Wall Oven 27x24x81 | Double Wall Oven 30x24x81 | Double Wall Oven 33x24x81 | Warming Drawer 30x24x34½ |

Base Cabinets – Blind Base Corner

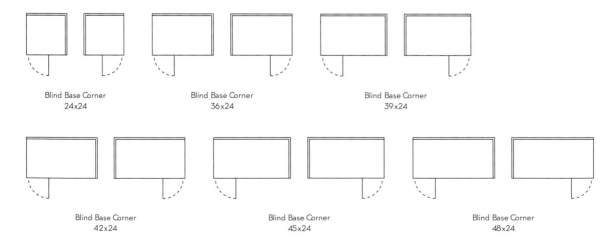

Blind Base Corner
24x24

Blind Base Corner
36x24

Blind Base Corner
39x24

Blind Base Corner
42x24

Blind Base Corner
45x24

Blind Base Corner
48x24

Standard Cabinet Height: 34½ inches.

Base Corner Cabinets

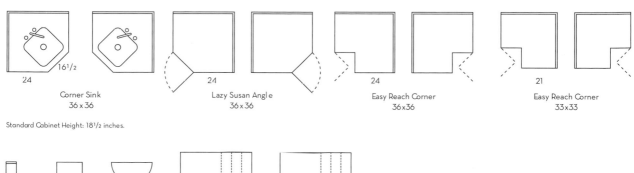

Corner Sink
36 x 36

Lazy Susan Angle
36 x 36

Easy Reach Corner
36 x 36

Easy Reach Corner
33 x 33

Standard Cabinet Height: 18½ inches.

Base Drawer
Cabinet
24 x 6

File Drawers
24 x 15

Penninsula
Base
12 x 24

Island
24 x 24
24 x 30
24 x 36
24 x 42

Island
30 x 24
30 x 30
30 x 36
30 x 42

Standard Cabinet Height is 34½ inches except for File Drawers, which is 28½ inches.

Open Shelf for Base End

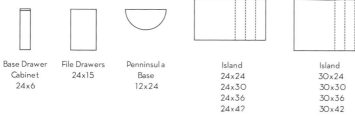

36 x 24

39 x 24

42 x 24

45 x 24

48 x 24

Standard Cabinet Height is 34½ inches.

Pantries

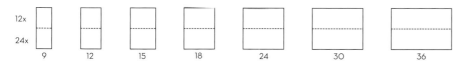

12x

24x

9

12

15

18

24

30

36

Standard Cabinet Heights: 84, 90, and 96 inches.

Refrigerators

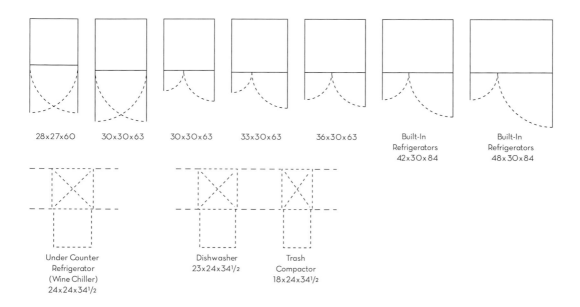

28 x 27 x 60

30 x 30 x 63

30 x 30 x 63

33 x 30 x 63

36 x 30 x 63

Built-In
Refrigerators
42 x 30 x 84

Built-In
Refrigerators
48 x 30 x 84

Under Counter
Refrigerator
(Wine Chiller)
24 x 24 x 34½

Dishwasher
23 x 24 x 34½

Trash
Compactor
18 x 24 x 34½

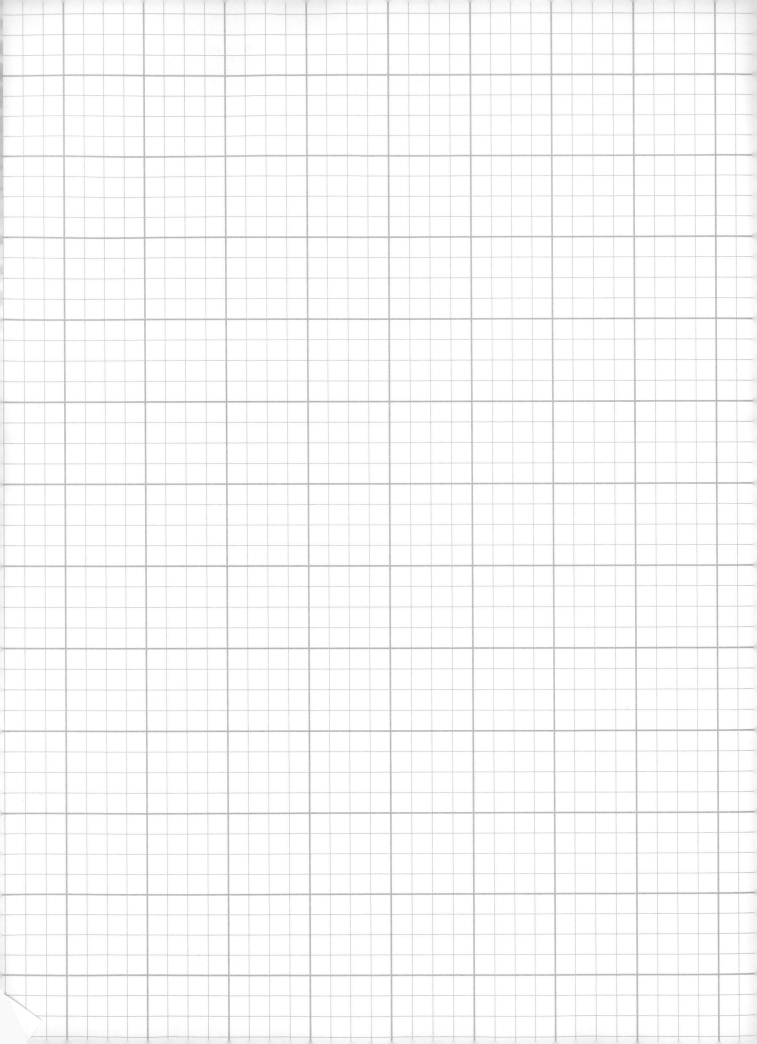

index